Anthony Hecht

in conversation with

Philip Hoy

Anthony Hecht

in conversation with

Philip Hoy

BETWEEN THE LINES BTL BETWEEN THE LINES

First published in 1999 by

BETWEEN THE LINES **BTL** BETWEEN THE LINES

9 Woodstock Road
London N4 3ET
UK

T :+44 (0)20 8374 5526 F :+44 (0)20 8374 5736 E-mail : btluk@aol.com
Website: http://www.interviews-with-poets.com

Second edition, corrected and reset, 2001
Third edition, including 31 additional illustrations, 2004

ISBN 1 903291 15 1

Design and typography by Philip Hoy

Printed and bound by Grafiche Dessi s.r.l.
Riva presso Chieri (TO), Italy

BTL publishes unusually wide-ranging and unusually deep-going interviews with some of today's most accomplished poets.

Some would deny that any useful purpose is served by putting to a writer questions which are not answered by his or her books. For them, what Yeats called 'the bundle of accident and incoherence that sits down to breakfast' is best left alone, not asked to interrupt its cornflakes, or to set aside its morning paper, while someone with a tape recorder inquires about its life, habits and attitudes.

If we do not share this view, it is not because we endorse Sainte-Beuve's dictum, *tel arbre, tel fruit — as the tree, so the fruit* — but because we understand what Geoffrey Braithwaite was getting at when the author of *Flaubert's Parrot* had him say:

> 'But if you love a writer, if you depend upon the drip-feed of his intelligence, if you want to pursue him and find him — despite edicts to the contrary — then it's impossible to know too much.'

Eleven other volumes are currently available, featuring, in order of publication, W.D. Snodgrass, Michael Hamburger, Anthony Thwaite, Donald Hall, Thom Gunn, Richard Wilbur, Seamus Heaney, Donald Justice, Ian Hamilton, Charles Simic and John Ashbery. Further details about these are given overleaf. Other volumes now being prepared will feature Peter Dale and Mark Strand.

As well as the interview, each of these volumes contains a sketch of the poet's life and career, a comprehensive bibliography, archival information, and a representative selection of quotations from the poet's critics and reviewers. More recent volumes also include uncollected poems. It is hoped that the results will be of interest to the lay reader and specialist alike.

— Other volumes from BTL —

W.D. Snodgrass
in conversation with
Philip Hoy

Michael Hamburger
in conversation with
Peter Dale

Anthony Thwaite
in conversation with
Peter Dale and Ian Hamilton

Donald Hall
in conversation with
Ian Hamilton

Thom Gunn
in conversation with
James Campbell

Richard Wilbur
in conversation with
Peter Dale

Seamus Heaney
in conversation with
Karl Miller

Donald Justice
in conversation with
Philip Hoy

Ian Hamilton
in conversation with
Dan Jacobson

Charles Simic
in conversation with
Michael Hulse

John Ashbery
in conversation with
Mark Ford

CONTENTS

LIST OF ILLUSTRATIONS

ACKNOWLEDGEMENTS

The editors would like to thank a number of people for their contributions to this volume.

For help with background and bibliographical research: Professor David Cesarani (Wiener Library, London), Jenny Entwistle (Oxford University Press, Oxford), Mark Hassall (Institute of Archaeology, University College, London), Lisa Joliffe (Harvard University Press, London), Suzanne Iaconetti (Harvard University Press, Boston), Helen Fallon (Dublin City University Library), Cheri Peters, (Sewanee Writers' Conference), and Lawrence Mielniczuk (Bodleian Library, University of Oxford).

For having read earlier drafts of the interview, and made many useful suggestions: Helen Hecht, Rodney Pybus and Charles Arthurs.

For the many photographs we have been able to feature in this edition: Dorothy Alexander, Benjamin Dimmitt, Jill Krementz, the late Rollie Mckenna, James R. Peters, the late William Stafford, the Prints and Photographs Division of the Library of Congress, the Department of Rare Books and Special Collections in the University of Rochester Library, the Deutsches Archäeologisches Institut, Rome.

For his help in getting many of these photographs to us: John F. Andrews.

For having supplied us with prints of most of the photographs we have used, as well as advising us on suitable captions: Anthony and Helen Hecht.

Anthony Hecht
Washington D.C., 2001

courtesy of the photographer, Philip Hoy ©

A Note on Anthony Hecht

Anthony Hecht was born in New York City in 1923, the first son of Melvyn Hahlo Hecht and Dorothea Hecht (née Holzman). His brother Roger, who would also become a poet, was born two and a half years later.

Hecht was educated at three of New York City's schools, and then, in 1940, enrolled as an undergraduate at Bard College, an experimental adjunct of Columbia University, situated at Annandale-on-Hudson. It was at Bard, while still a freshman, that he made up his mind to become a poet, having been introduced to the work of Wallace Stevens, T.S. Eliot, W.H. Auden, Dylan Thomas and others by an inspiring teacher called Lawrence Leighton.

WWII obliged Hecht to give up his studies before graduating. At first, it looked as though he would be assigned to do intelligence work, but the special training programme he was inducted into was cancelled at the last minute, with the result that Hecht found himself *en route* to Europe, and some of the bloodiest fighting of the war. Any reader curious to know why the subject of cruelty recurs so frequently in Hecht's work need look no further than this period in his life for the explanation.

After the war was over, Hecht – whose B.A. had been awarded *in absentia* – took advantage of the G.I. Bill of Rights and went to Kenyon College in Ohio, where he resumed his studies, this time under the supervision of John Crowe Ransom, one of the most gifted men of letters of the day. It was Ransom who gave Hecht his first English classes to teach, thereby setting him on the path to a long and distinguished career as a professor; and it was Ransom, too, as editor of *The Kenyon Review*, who published some of Hecht's earliest poems, thereby setting him on the path to an even longer and still more distinguished career as a poet.

In the fifty years since his days as a student at Kenyon, Hecht has published seventeen books of poetry, three books of criticism, and a large number of essays, reviews, discussion pieces, forewords, prefaces and introductions. He has also done acclaimed work as a translator and editor.

Hecht's endeavours have been rewarded with a string of prestigious prizes and awards, amongst them: the Prix de Rome (1951), the Brandeis University Creative Arts Award (1965), the Pulitzer Prize for Poetry and the Russell Loines Award (1968), the Bollingen Prize in Poetry (1983), the Librex-Guggenheim Eugenio Montale Award (1984), the Harriet Monroe Award (1987), the Ruth B. Lilly Poetry Prize (1988), the Tanning Prize (1997), the Corrington Award (1997), and the Poetry Society of America's Frost Medal (2000).

Other honours to come Hecht's way included two Guggenheim Fellowships (1954 and 1959), *The Hudson Review* Fellowship (1958), two Ford Foundation Fellowships (1960 and 1968), a Rockefeller Fellowship (1967), a Fulbright Professorship in Brazil (1969), an Honorary Fellowship with the Academy of American Poets (1969), Membership of the National Institute of Arts and Letters (1979), Chancellorship (1971) and Chancellorship Emeritus (1995) of the Academy of American Poets, and Trusteeship of the American Academy in Rome (1983). He was also Consultant in Poetry to the Library of Congress in Washington D.C. (1982-1984).

As well as the B.A. he was awarded by Bard College in 1944, and the M.A. he was awarded by Columbia University in 1950, Hecht has received honorary doctorates from Bard College (1970), Georgetown University (1981), Towson State University, Maryland (1983) and the University of Rochester (1987).

Hecht has three sons, two by his first marriage, to Patricia Harris, which ended in divorce in 1961, and one by his second, to Helen D'Alessandro – the author of several renowned cookery books, and a successful interior designer – with whom he lives in Washington D.C.

A NOTE ON PHILIP HOY

Philip Hoy was born in London in 1952, and educated at the Universities of York and Leeds. He has a Ph.D in Philosophy, a subject he taught for many years, first in the UK and then overseas. Hoy is executive editor of Between The Lines and also manages the recently founded Waywiser Press. His most recent publications are *W.D. Snodgrass in Conversation with Philip Hoy* (BTL, 1998) and *Donald Justice in Conversation with Philip Hoy* (BTL, 2001). He lives in north London with the architect Evelina Francia.

A Conversation with Anthony Hecht

In July 1998 a list of almost one hundred questions – some of them quite long and involved – was sent to Anthony Hecht in Washington. The accompanying letter said, 'It would be helpful if we could have your answers by the end of the year,' but, because it was felt that this might be unrealistic, went on: 'if you need longer, all you have to do is let us know.' The interviewer was therefore quite taken aback when the bulky typescript containing Hecht's answers to these questions – it ran to more than sixty A4 pages – arrived in London just a few *weeks*, rather than a few *months*, later.

With the typescript came a typically generous letter: 'I have had much pleasure writing my part of this interview. So much so that, while I abandoned my typescript of it when we went abroad for two weeks to Italy, it haunted me enough that I made notes for it in Venice, and returned home with a number of touches that I think may give pleasure.' More generous still was the offer to treat this as the *beginning*, rather than the *end*, of the conversation: 'I imagine my replies will prompt further questions from you. And of course you may find some of my comments unsatisfactory. Perhaps we should regard the enclosed pages as a "first draft", subject to as much revision as you think is warranted.'

What you are about to read is in fact the fourth complete draft, arrived at after an exchange of over fifty faxes and letters, which came to an end in May 1999.

Perhaps I could begin by asking you to say something about your childhood — who your parents were, how big the family was, where you lived, and what the general circumstances (economic, religious, cultural) of your upbringing were?

I was born into an upper-middle-class family in New York City in 1923. My parents were of German-Jewish background, though born in America, as were their parents. The Jewish part of their heritage was something they felt awkward about: both proud and ashamed. The shame was the kind engendered by conventional anti-Semitism, and the social ostracism experienced by virtually all Jews in a gentile society (I don't believe their families had been driven to emigrate by pogroms; I think they came to America because in the mid-nineteenth century it was a legendary land of hope and promise). The pride was based on a fantasy that the Jews were somehow all 'brilliant' as a race (a conviction they must have realized they were both exceptions to), and that many of the greatest men and women, if the truth were but known, were actually Jews. They cherished the idea that these included Charlie Chaplin and Copernicus and others equally unlikely. (This resembles the corresponding belief among homosexuals that all those they admire are closet gays.) But they were not very observing Jews. My mother's family attended synagogue on Rosh Hashanah, though more for social than any other reasons; and we went to the home of some aunt or uncle, never seen on any other occasion, to celebrate the Passover. My father, an uncommonly superstitious man, declared himself a complete atheist. My only sibling, my brother, was born two and a half years after me, and was epileptic virtually from birth. My mother never went to college (partly because it was then assumed that ladies of her class needed only domestic graces) and my father went to Harvard, but was obliged to drop out when his own father suddenly went blind, and required someone to take over the family business.

And the name Hecht? Where does that come from?

Hecht in German means *pike*, the fish. My father's family seems to have come from Bamberg, a Bavarian city which I happened to pass through with my army unit during WWII. My father assumed that his ancestors were fishermen.

How would you describe your childhood? The opening lines of 'Apprehensions', if they're read as autobiographical, suggest that it could not have been very happy:

> *A grave and secret malady of my brother's,*
> *The stock exchange, various grown-up shames,*
> *The white emergency of hospitals,*
> *Inquiries from the press, such coups de thèâtre*
> *Upon a stage from which I was excluded*
> *Under the rubric of 'benign neglect'*
> *Had left me pretty much to my own devices*
> *(My own stage was about seven years old)*
> *Except for a Teutonic governess*
> *Replete with the curious thumb-print of her race,*
> *That special relish for inflicted pain.*

Am I right in seeing this as autobiographical? And if so, am I right in thinking that yours was a fairly unhappy childhood?

You're right on both counts. The poem is autobiographical, and my childhood was indeed unhappy. The reasons, at least some of them, have been mercifully clouded by time and my age. Perhaps it should begin with my brother's affliction. He was not only epileptic; he limped, he had a semi-paralyzed right hand, and eyesight so poor that as a child he was made to exercise his eyes every day for long periods with a stereopticon, the focusing of which was meant to limber the muscles of his eyes and correct his tendency to be cross-eyed. He also had a door-frame gymnasium with a crossbar to strengthen his arms. He was quite young when he began psychotherapy for his seizures (only when he was fully grown did they find the right medications that could control these) though he was taking some sort of pills almost from the start. His terrible handicap was cruel in itself, and had the curious effect of making my mother feel quite martyred, a disposition that increased throughout the length of her life, as did the grounds of her aggrievedness. Not that there were no serious causes for this, at least at first. My father, as I said, had to quit college to take over his father's business, The New England Enamel Company, which manufactured household utensils. He hated business and was not good at it. In the course of my lifetime he lost every cent he had, not once but three times; and not only his own money but that of friendly investors, who came to regard him as either a crook or stupid. Each time this happened he attempted suicide. In my second year of college, I was suddenly sent home because my brother's shrink believed that my father, who had disappeared (a matter of which I knew nothing) was planning to kidnap me (for what purpose I can't imagine, though my father was really a near hysteric, so I suppose he might have done any-thing). His financial difficulties were, it must be pointed out, not all of his own making. When I was six the stock market collapsed, and I can re-member seeing on New York sidewalks the bodies of those, covered for decency's sake with blankets, who had thrown themselves from windows. Our own condition went down noticeably in the world, though we were never seriously in want. Each time my father lost his shirt (and the frock coats of others) my mother's family bailed him out. But her rage about this, as about other matters, came close to unhinging her. In 1950 I was on a fellowship in Rome; my parents came through, though significantly not at the same time. My mother came first. She told me that my father's job (she had by this time demanded that he no longer run his own busi-ness, but instead accept a salaried job, and work under someone else's direction) was not 'real' in that it was entirely subsidized by her parents, the money being paid to the employer by her own father. She went on to say that she planned to divorce my father, and that immediately his salary would cease. The point was not simply that he would be penniless once again but that the discovery that he had not been holding a real job but was being supported by his in-laws would so humiliate him that he would 'probably commit suicide.' I remember being told this in the lobby of the Hassler Hotel over cocktails. I could see that she was in a strange state, but that didn't mean that she wasn't telling the truth. My father arrived a day or so after she left. I felt that unless I told him what I had just learned he might hear it first from a lawyer, and act as my mother seemed to intend. So I told him what she said, and he claimed it was wholly untrue, which, as it turned out, was the case. The main point, however, is that as a child I regarded my family as especially vulnerable to financial and social downward mobility. I remember going to increasingly more modest places to buy clothing, restricting vacations to shabbier beach resorts.

What sort of education did you receive prior to entering University?

After a peaceful era in kindergarten, I attended three different schools in New York. First, the Dalton School, where my schoolmates included three children of Leopold Stokowski, and the first girl I was ever to have a crush on (an unspoken, smothered passion) whose name, to my chagrin and outrage, was Toni. I don't know what I learned there. It was very permissive. From there I was sent to the Collegiate School, a place Dickensianly different. Here I encountered discipline for the first time. There was a French teacher named Sueur, who used to hurl blackboard erasers at students for whatever lapse he thought merited such treatment; and he liked to swat a student's open palm with the flat of a ruler a specified number of times depending on the infraction. He was a French sadist, carefully to be distinguished from the German variety. The Latin and math teachers were severe but kind. I sang in some sort of glee club and, the school being of Dutch Presbyterian denomination, there were chapel services every morning before classes, which I enjoyed because it postponed the humiliation of my poor class performances. Then, at last, I went to the Horace Mann School for Boys, in Riverdale, which involved over an hour by subway and bus each way. This meant rising long before my parents, and a late return home. My teachers there were unimaginative, except for one who went crazy and had to be institutionalized. Most of them had conventional minds, which were sometimes also small. There was a history teacher named Martin who hated Roosevelt, and, only slightly less, me. He avowed in class, before all my classmates, that I did not deserve to go to college, and that he would do everything in his power to prevent me from going. The wonder of it is that I surprised everyone, myself included, by getting honours in mathematics from a gentle old man named Callahan. But my record, on the whole, was not good. I was wretched in chemistry. The English courses were stunningly uninspired, not least one taught by a man who thought himself 'inspirational' because he went into raptures about Shelley's 'Skylark'. He was never able to explain what was so good about it — just that he thought it utterly intoxicating. He was an early prefiguration of Robin Williams in *The Dead Poets Society*, a film premised on the notion that if you behaved oddly and danced around on desktops you were one of the initiate, and a certified resident of Parnassus. The utterly unconvincing behaviour of this teacher was not easy to cope with; but what truly bewildered me was that all the other members of my class seemed to go along with him. They struck me as either fools or hypocrites. I had no good friends there.

Since you did not do very well at school, how was it that you ended up going to Bard?

At the time I went to Bard it was not a difficult place to get into. My father had dreams that I would follow him to Harvard, but that was out of the question, and my interview there, carried out at his initiative, was humiliating.

Bard was quite a small institution at that time, and I have seen it described as 'an experimental adjunct' to Columbia University. Can you say in what way or ways it was 'experimental'?

Bard, founded mid-nineteenth century by one John Bard as an Episcopal college named St. Stephen's, had been taken over at some point by Columbia University, and used to test and put into practice the educational ideas of Columbia's great philosopher, John Dewey. It had been at the beginning, and remained, a very small school, run along what had come to be called 'progressive' lines. I entered in 1940, that is to say, about a year and a half before the United States entered the war. Being a part of Columbia, it offered a Columbia degree. But because it was small, with a very high faculty/student ratio, it was expensive to run, and the war provided the university with an excuse to end the experiment. Bard became independent and went co-ed, not on principle, but because without Columbia's support, it needed women, during and just after the war, to make ends meet. It was experimental in that it allowed more than traditional freedom in selecting majors and courses. I was a music major for a while, before shifting to literature. Grading was done on what were called 'criteria sheets', which contained extended statements and assessments by all the faculty with whom one studied. Often this revealed as much about the teacher as the student.

You were 17 when you entered Bard. Did you leave home at that time, or was that to come later?

21

I went to live at college.

How quickly was it borne in on you that you were not, academically speaking, the ugly duckling you had been led to believe?

At college, for the first time, I made real friends. None of my school classmates had meant much to me, though I rather liked Jack Kerouac, who was in my high school class, and won a football scholarship to Columbia. I not only found I liked my fellow students at college but a good number of my teachers. My grades initially were mediocre, but they grew better with time, and I won some awards.

How was your progress at Bard greeted by your parents?

I don't seem to recall that my parents took much interest in what happened to me at college, with one exception. They were understandably too preoccupied with more urgent matters — my poor brother's illness, domestic hostility, financial travails. The exception occurred when, having fallen head over heels in love with poetry for the first time in my life, I came home for some holiday and cheerfully, naively announced to my parents that I planned to become a poet. This was greeted with uncharacteristic silence, which should have warned me. I expected at least some token resistance. It turned out that my parents were far more alarmed than I could have guessed, and decided to call in outside help. Among their friends at this period was the later much-celebrated Dr. Seuss, the cartoonist, whose name was Ted Geisel. Ted and his wife were guests at dinner the next time I came home. Initially I suspected nothing, but after dinner Ted put his hand on my shoulder in an avuncular way that made me cautious, and asked, 'Well, Tony, what do you want to do when you grow up?' The question itself was a dead give-away. I think I was still a freshman at the time, and there was no reason for anyone my age to have planned that far ahead; so there had to be a tip-off. I briefly debated with myself about how to respond, but quickly concluded that all was known, and that in any case I might as well speak about my deep enthusiasm. So I said I hoped to become a poet. Ted said, 'That's a fine ambition. And let me tell you what I think you should do first of all. I think you should read the life of Joseph Pulitzer.' I knew nothing about Pulitzer at that age, except that he was a newspaper man. What that had to do with poetry I couldn't guess, but I shrewdly suspected that something in that biography would be highly discouraging, so I instantly resolved never to read it, and I never have.

*You had amongst your professors at Bard a man by the name of Law-
rence Leighton, whom you credit with 'having imparted a sense of ur-
gency and purpose to the study of poetry.' Can you say something about
Professor Leighton, and his part in your development?*

It was Larry Leighton who aroused my delight in poetry. He was a strange
man, gentle but in some ways forbidding. For one thing, he was a com-
plete alcoholic, more addicted than anyone I have ever known. I took a
class with him, held in his rooms, with perhaps five or six other students
at, I would guess, nine or ten in the morning. We would regularly have to
rouse him from bed, and pour half a glass of straight gin into his tooth-
brush glass for him before, clad in nothing but a bathrobe, he would even
be able to talk. He was also a quite unembarrassed homosexual, who
found an all-male college much to his liking. He was often slyly or even
boldly provocative about the homoerotic in poetry. He took obvious de-
light in calling our attention to Gaveston's speech in Edward II that be-
gins, 'I must have wanton poets, pleasant wits ...' What this had to do
with a course in modern poetry is not easy to say, but he was always
wide-ranging in his remarks, and we had learned to expect almost any-
thing, not least because of the breadth of his learning. Often he was hop-
ing for more knowing sexual sophistication than I was able to summon.
When he pointed to Hart Crane's line, from *The Bridge*, ' ... and love / A
burnt match, skating in a urinal — ', he would eye us carefully for signs of
smirking comprehension, which, as it happened, I was unable to come
up with, since I completely missed the merit he found in those words.
Nevertheless, he was a marvellous teacher, more widely read than any-
one I had yet encountered, and with a seemingly limitless enthusiasm for
literary works. More precisely, there was nothing formulaic in his responses
to poetry. My school teachers had been no more than the conduits of
received ideas, not unlike the teachers Philip Larkin encountered at Ox-
ford, who commended Dryden for 'the complete mastery of his instru-
ment' and his ability 'perfectly to express an idea.' That sort of stuff is
meaningless and unhelpful. But Larry Leighton was often talking to us
about poets so new, and so little mauled over by critical comment, that
his reactions were almost as fresh as our own. In 1940 or '41 I bought
Eliot's *Collected Poems: 1909-1935*, the copy I still own. I bought Dylan
Thomas's *Twenty-Five Poems*, large quantities of Auden, the second edi-
tion of Hopkins, Stevens's *Harmonium*, and much else. About all these
poets he was lively, conjectural, imaginative and open to dissenting opin-
ion. Later in the course of things he organized what he called 'The Blithe
Spirit Society', to which one was bidden because 'bird thou never wert'.

It was an invitation issued to students he found attractive to come to his rooms and drink as heavily as they wished in the evenings. I never went.

Although it wasn't until your freshman year that you fell in love with poetry, you'd been writing it for quite a while. Do you remember what prompted your earliest poems? Can you say what they were about?

I have mercifully forgotten my earliest work. It was far worse than Eliot's. A good deal of it was light verse, though there was one serious poem prompted by one of my father's collapses.

You've described your three years as an undergraduate at Bard as 'unquestionably the happiest ... of [your] life up to that time.' How did it feel when, three years into your studies, aged 20, you were drafted into the army, and sent off to fight in the war? Was it something you'd been dreading?

I admit with shame that I felt neither brave nor patriotic. I was profoundly scared. I had, as you say, just encountered something like happiness for the first time in my life, and I was now required to give it up, and perhaps my life as well. My reading had become so important to me that when I finally went off to the army reception centre I brought with me a paperback collection of some Shakespeare plays, an anthology of poetry, some Joyce, and a volume of Spinoza. It wasn't until about two weeks into basic training that I was allowed enough leisure to ferret out one of those books, expecting to slip easily into the receptive appreciation I enjoyed at college. But the words lay blank and flat on the page. It was like reading a telephone directory. The combination of fatigue and the numbing effect of close-order drill, along with other dehumanizing methods of military training, had all but lobotomized me. I feared I would never be able to read anything with pleasure again, should I even survive. It was a terrifying kind of pre-death. In the end, all those faculties returned about six or eight months after I got out.

You saw action in France, Germany and Czechoslovakia, and witnessed the deaths of a great many of your comrades. How did you cope with this?

There is much about this I have never spoken about, and never will. My father made a foolish and pitiful attempt to get me discharged while I was in training in Missouri with the 97th Infantry Division, the outfit with which

I went overseas. He somehow managed to inform officers of the division of his own mental breakdowns, and to imply that I was subject to the same frailties. I was called away from a bivouac to be interviewed by a military shrink. When I figured out what was going on, I realized I had only to put on an act in order to get discharged on what the army called a Section Eight, or 'mental' grounds. I really felt that my life that morning was in my own hands. At the same time, I felt unwilling to fake, and ashamed of what my father had done. I confined myself to acknowledging that I hated the army — like *Catch 22*, this was regarded as a sign of mental soundness — and refusing to address the interrogating officer as 'Sir,' an act of mild but, to me, meaningful insubordination.

Did you make a good soldier?

Not by any real standards. I was honourably discharged at the end of things, and I did not disobey any orders, though once I was genuinely tempted to. My company had been pinned down by very heavy enemy fire in Germany. Our company commander was a fool, wholly incapable of any initiative, who slavishly obeyed commands, however uninformed or ill-considered, from battalion or regimental HQ, and without regard to the safety or capacity of his own troops. (He was later awarded a Silver Star for action that took place on a day when he was behind the lines being treated for dysentery.) Anyway, on this day when we were hopelessly kept flat on the ground by superior fire-power, some idiot at an upper echelon, far behind the lines and blissfully unaware of our situation re-garding the enemy (though probably eager to keep all forward move-ments abreast of one another to protect all flanks) ordered my company to move forward, and the captain ordered us to ready ourselves, though there would have been nothing but total annihilation in prospect. At the last second, higher command called for artillery, which turned the trick. And as we slowly rose from prone positions, I confessed to my platoon commander, a second lieutenant just about my age, that if the order to advance had not been countermanded I was very unsure whether I would have obeyed. 'Of course you would have,' he replied, but with a look that meant a great deal. He fully understood how foolish such a com-mand would have been at the time, but as an officer, whose duty was to set an example, he knew that he would have had to obey.

You served with the Infantry Division which discovered Flossenbürg, a concentration camp in the Bavarian forest, close to the Czech border. It's not as notorious as its neighbour, Buchenwald — it rates a mention in several of the history books just because it was there that Dietrich Bonhoeffer was murdered, a week before the liberation — but it was a major camp, and one wouldn't have to read a book like Robert Abzug's Inside the Vicious Heart: Americans and the Liberation of Nazi Concentration Camps *to understand how devastating an experience it must have been for young G.I.s like you, though you must already have witnessed some pretty awful things. Can you say anything about this event, and its effect on you?*

Flossenbürg was an annex of Buchenwald. It was both an extermination camp and a slave-labour camp, where prisoners were made to manufacture Messerschmitts at a factory right within the perimeter of the camp. When we arrived, the SS personnel had, of course, fled. Prisoners were dying at the rate of 500 a day from typhus. Since I had the rudiments of French and German, I was appointed to interview such French prisoners as were well enough to speak, in the hope of securing evidence against those who ran the camp. Later, when some of these were captured, I presented them with the charges levelled against them, translating their denials or defences back into French for the sake of their accusers, in an attempt to get to the bottom of what was done and who was responsible. The place, the suffering, the prisoners' accounts were beyond comprehension. For years after I would wake shrieking. I must add an important point: after the war I read widely in Holocaust literature, and I can no longer separate my anger and revulsion at what I really saw from what I later came to learn.

Were there any aspects of life in the army that you valued?

Not at the time, certainly. I found that all the officers I encountered from the rank of captain on up were contemptible and often ignorant, swaggering in the full vigour of their incapacity, and this was true up to as high a level as division commander, which I had the opportunity of observing. While I came to this conclusion independently and on the basis of personal experience, I find that I'm not the only one to have held such views. Allow me, if you will, a small literary flourish. In *Joseph Andrews* Fielding writes about Nature, personified as a goddess of great powers, who equips creatures with a cranial cavity for the brains and their rational government of ordinary men, 'whereas,' Fielding goes on to remark, 'those ingredients being entirely useless to persons of the heroic calling, she hath an opportunity of thickening the bone so as to make it less subject to any impression, or liable to be cracked or broken; and indeed, in some who are predestined to command armies and empires, she is supposed sometimes to make that part perfectly solid.' It would have been a convenient balance and fitting irony to say that, by contrast, the ordinary draftees with no military ambitions or careers, were often good and generous people, and this is what I believed at first. But a few days of heavy front-line combat changed my attitude in a terrible way. We had already suffered some severe casualties from enemy mortars and land mines. These first casualties and deaths came to us as a rude shock; our friends and comrades, with whom we had trained, undergone real privations and endured grave dangers were now legless, armless, or dead. So the mood of the company was shaken when, one morning, we found ourselves hugging the ground at the crest of a hill, in the shadow of trees, looking out across a green field that dipped shallowly in the middle before rising to a small height not far away, and behind which German troops were lobbing mortar shells at us. We fired back, and the exchange went on for a while, until at last the enemy simply stopped firing. This could, of course, have been preliminary to something else, a trick, anything. We remained exactly where we were. And then, to my astonishment, a small group of German women, perhaps five or six, leading small children by the hand, and with white flags of surrender fixed to staves and broom-handles, came up over the far crest and started walking slowly toward us, waving their white flags back and forth. They came slowly, the children retarding their advance. They had to descend the small incline that lay between their height and ours. When they were about half way, and about to climb the slope leading to our position, two of our machine guns opened up and slaughtered the whole group. Not long after we were able to take the enemy position, from which all their troops had withdrawn. For the rest of the day there was much loud and insistent talk about that morning's slaughter, all intended as justification. 'They might have had bombs on them.' 'They might have had some radio devices to direct German artillery toward us.' Things like that. This was all due to the plain panic of soldiers newly exposed to combat, due also to guilt, to frustrated fury at the casualties we had suffered. In any case, what I saw that morning was, except for Flossenbürg, the greatest trauma of the war — and, believe me, I saw a lot of terrible things. But that morning left me without the least vestige of patriotism or national pride. And when I hear empty talk about that war having been a 'good war', as contrasted with, say, Vietnam, I maintain a fixed silence. The men in my company, under ordinary circumstances, were not vicious or criminal, but I no longer felt close to any of them. Battle, which is supposed to bring fellow soldiers together, failed to do that. As for whether there were any aspects of army life that I valued, I'd have to maintain my equivocal posture. The army put me in what may be the best physical shape I would ever enjoy, and as though to annul this benefit, it taught me to smoke. And I went on smoking, addictively, for thirty-five years.

You said at the beginning of this interview that your parents felt awkward about the Jewish part of their heritage. Did you feel awkward about it too?

In my generation anti-Semitism was widespread and very common, scarcely to be avoided, and indeed regarded as a sign of cultivation on the part of not a few. One of my earliest literary heroes, Eliot, wrote lines I found personally wounding. So did Pound, and too many others to mention, including Dickens. It was virtually a badge of polite society. It also infuses ineradicably some parts of the Gospels, and was almost doctrinal among Catholics of my acquaintance, one of whom, regarding herself as a friend of mine, explained to me that I was 'invincibly ignorant' by way of cheering me up about my hopes for salvation. What I saw at Flossenbürg and what I read about the camps only increased my sense of unrelieved horror. To be exposed to this kind of thing, in literature, in religious doctrine, in personal relationships, over a long period of time can have a very potent effect.

When did the effect begin to wear off?

Curiously, when the war and all its horrors were over and publicly exposed, a number of 'intellectuals', Mary McCarthy and Robert Lowell among them, bravely made public the fact that there were Jews in their family backgrounds. Needless to say, when your name is McCarthy or Lowell you are not likely to be exposed to much in the way of anti-Semitism. But in time I came to feel an awed reverence for what the Jews of Europe had undergone, a sense of marvel at the hideousness of what they had been forced to endure. I came to feel that it was important to be worthy of their sacrifices, to justify my survival in the face of their misery and extinction, and slowly I began to shed my shame at being Jewish.

In the interview you did with J.D. McClatchy, you drew on a distinction made by William James in The Varieties of Religious Experience, *classifying yourself as* sick-souled *rather than* healthy-minded. *To quote James — though in a way which hardly does justice to the richness of his thinking on this matter — the healthy-minded 'live habitually on the sunny side of their misery-line,' while the sick-souled 'live beyond it, in dark-*

ness and apprehension'. Would you say that your wartime experiences were responsible for your being sick-souled, or was this trait already apparent in your younger self, as the poem from which I have already quoted strongly suggests?

Yes, I suspect I am a 'depressive' type, without even the consolation of enjoying intervals of manic highs. This is not a condition in which I pride myself, or for which I think myself entitled to pity. I have seen enough suffering in the world — in my own family, as well as during the war — to know that others have lived far worse lives than mine. But I do believe that some are blessed with a temperament that inclines instinctively to cheerfulness. And I admire and envy them. James singled out Emerson and Whitman as specimens of this type. Among contemporary poets I would hasten to add Edward Hirsch. One of his books was called *Wild Gratitude*, and, of a sequence of poems from a later book, *On Love*, he wrote, 'I decided to call a symposium on love. I would invite only those poets I was most interested in hearing from; ... I began by developing a shocking squib from Baudelaire's *Intimate Journals*. When I moved on to Heine speaking from his mattress-grave, I realized that some "lectures" would be turning into love poems. The forms would be a form of praise, a fever psalm. Suddenly, I was setting sail for happiness ...'

I know that sequence of Hirsch's, and the explanatory note: John Hollander included them in his The Best American Poetry: 1998.

It would be churlish not to find this attitude of Hirsch's admirable; but I myself am not of that ilk, and there's nothing I can do about it. Donald Davie once wrote a particularly wounding review of a book of mine (as he had done of one of my earlier books as well). This later book was titled *The Venetian Vespers*, and the title poem, a grim one, was not about me but about someone I knew. Davie chose to review my book in tandem with one by the admirable poet, Josephine Miles, whose work I had long regarded with great respect. Davie wrote, 'Anthony Hecht is likely to be the sufferer from the chance that has thrown him and Jo Miles together.' Let me interrupt to say that it wasn't chance but Davie who threw us together. He could have reviewed us separately or omitted my book entirely. But for purposes of his review I became his whipping boy. 'It is very bad luck,' he continues, 'for any of us to be reviewed along with her. For she is in a muted way a sort of Helen Keller heroine, arthritically crippled through most or all of her adult life, who has surmounted her afflictions so as to live a busy and productive life as a teacher and a scholar, as well as a poet. When we add that it is she, thus afflicted, who in her poems is nearly always cheerful and sunny and serene, Hecht's misfortune becomes obvious; because on the whole the range of moods in his work is from dark gray to savage black. In mere justice to him, therefore, one would prefer not to allude to Ms. Miles's disabilities, the more so since she has never paraded them, to make capital out of them.' This is but a small part of a review that is uncomplicatedly vicious. I must add that I never reviewed any of his work, spoke or wrote unfavourably of him at any time. In fact, I admired a critical book of his called *Articulate Energy*.

It was while you were in the army that you met Robie Macauley, who had enrolled at Kenyon College in 1938, and been a student of John Crowe Ransom's. He'd also shared a house with Robert Lowell, Randall Jarrell, Peter Taylor and John Thompson. How did this meeting with Macauley come about? Was it pure happenstance?

Robie was a member of the Counterintelligence Corps, to which I was temporarily attached because of my sketchy knowledge of French and German. We got on well, and liked many of the same classical composers.

After leaving Europe, you spent some time in occupied Japan. What did your duties there involve? And how did you react to the dislocation which removal to this part of the world must have involved?

In Japan I worked in a public relations unit of my division, which was on occupation duty just north of Tokyo. Our job was to write 'news items' that might be picked up by American wire services interested in local colour and which would put the occupying forces in a favourable light. It was quite shameless, hypocritical work, and therefore perfectly consistent with everything I had ever known about the army. I rather liked the Japanese I encountered. There was, of course, a language barrier, though there were times when I had a translator at my disposal. The Japanese seemed remarkably polite and shy, quite different from the Germans. And their manifest poverty was deeply touching.

You were discharged from the army in '46, your B.A. having been awarded in absentia. You then went to Kenyon, where, I think I'm right in saying, you spent a year. How difficult was it, adjusting from life as a soldier to life as a student?

Not as difficult as I might have feared. Returning home after being discharged was a challenge. I was drunk for two weeks. The real problems set in later. I had no goals or aims, and would have been lost had it not been for the G.I. Bill of Rights that allowed me to return to academic life, which was the only happy life I'd known. I went to Kenyon at the recommendation of Robie, who also advised me to read some of Ransom's work before I went, which I did. Kenyon gave no graduate degree, and I already had been awarded a B.A. from Bard, partly on the basis of language studies I had been assigned by the army, which had sent me to Carleton College in Minnesota for, I think, twenty-seven weeks. So I entered Kenyon as a 'special student', which meant I was not a degree candidate. Not long after I arrived a member of the English department got sick, and because I was marginally older than the undergraduates, and had a degree in English, they asked me if I would be willing to take over a freshman English course. I was interviewed by Mr Ransom himself, who was then my teacher. He was a courtly and gentle man, and among the questions he asked me was whether I had any teaching experience whatever. I was on the point of saying no, when it occurred to me that I actually did, though I didn't think it very pertinent. While I was at Bard the war was in progress, and many faculty as well as students were being called up. Like many other colleges, Bard had a government-sponsored program providing special training for the army and navy, mostly in math. The math teacher finally was called up, and for a panicked interval it was feared that the whole navy program would dissolve, which the college could ill-afford. The only faculty member deemed even remotely qualified was the man in economics, Franco Modigliani (who later won the economics Nobel Prize). Franco felt that the kind of math the navy wanted was too far back in his past to dredge up. But it wasn't remote for me, and so, though I was myself an undergraduate attending classes, I taught solid geometry and trigonometry under Franco's benign supervision for about three months, and neither Franco nor the navy ever expressed any dissatisfaction. When I told this to Ransom, thinking it could not be more irrelevant to teaching English, he was gratified, feeling that an interest in literature ought not to be divorced from other kinds of knowledge and experience. And so I was invited to teach the course, and hastily inducted into the faculty by the dean of the college, who informed me that there was no anti-Semitism to be feared at Kenyon, witness the solitary presence on the faculty of one Dr Salomon, who taught in the divinity school. I would have enjoyed punching him in the face; but I greatly liked and respected Ransom, and was enthusiastic about tackling the teaching job. And indeed this started me on the way to my means of subsistence for the rest of my life.

What did you read of John Crowe Ransom's before you arrived at Ohio? And what impression did it make on you?

I've written an essay on this topic which would be hard to condense. It was published in a book called *Masters: Portraits of Great Teachers* and included essays on Christian Gauss, Alfred North Whitehead, Nadia Boulanger, Hannah Arendt, C.S. Lewis and I.A. Richards, among others, by the likes of Edmund Wilson, Sidney Hook, Kenneth Lynn and Gerald Graff. I can only say that Ransom's prose astonished me, coming to it as I did from prior experience in reading the critical work of Eliot, Blackmur, Richards, Empson and Wilson. Where they were usually efficiently expository, he was diffident, cunning, wittily reserved, and ceremonious. And his poems were filled with archaisms that I had assumed modernity had buried forever. It took me quite a while to adjust my reading habits.

Can you say something about Ransom's classes, and their impact on you? If you had to pinpoint one major lesson he had to teach you, what would it be?

Back to my essay. I hope you won't mind my quoting a few sentences of my own, since they seem relevant. 'I find it difficult in retrospect to say exactly what it was one learned from Mr. Ransom, to point to particular notions or propositions. One found it possible, and sometimes necessary, to disagree with him — private, interior disagreements about details in the interpretation of poems, even of general philosophic premises — without losing any respect for him by such silent dissent. For one learned from him, not facts or positions, but a posture of the mind and spirit, a humanity and courtesy, a manly considerateness that inhabited his work as it did his person. And one learned to pay a keen attention to poetic detail.'

There's a letter from Randall Jarrell to Robert Penn Warren, in which he says how much more enjoyable he finds discussing aesthetic matters with Ransom than 'politics and freeing the slaves.' That was in 1935, and by the time you got to know Ransom his days as a conservative social theorist were quite a long way behind him; but I wonder, did you know anything of this side of the man? And if so, what did you make of it?

When I first knew Ransom I was aware that he had been a Southern Agrarian and a Fugitive, and that these were, in the eyes of many, honourable and regional as well as cultural allegiances. But it was not until many years later, and after Ransom's death, that I got around to reading the group manifesto, *I'll Take My Stand* (a title borrowed from the rather defiant anthem, *Dixie* – 'In Dixieland I'll take my stand, to live and die in Dixie.') Twelve contributors included Allen Tate, Andrew Lytle, Robert Penn Warren as well as Ransom. They believed they were advocating a tradition championed in the past by the likes of Cobbett, Ruskin and Carlyle, a mode of life resistant to capitalist industrialism, and predicated on a rural, land-owning, farming economy. Such ideas, under the rubric of economic distributism, had also been embraced by Chesterton and Belloc, who found them enunciated in the political encyclicals of Pope Leo XIII. In essence (and in the words of Belloc's biographer, A.N. Wilson), this came down to the doctrine that 'every man should own three acres and a cow. It was an anti-industrial, anti-capitalist, anti-modern view' which held that a person 'who earns almost no money but owns his own land, burns his own peat, grows his own potatoes and milks his own cow is a freer creature than a clerk or factory hand who might earn ten times more money, but is compelled to work for somebody else, and to live in a rented or a leased house, and to be dependent on shopkeepers for his sustenance.' Eliot, in his reactionary lectures, *After Strange Gods*, commended the Southern Agrarians on their stance. There is something wistful and touching about the manifesto itself and the society it envisions, not one of the contributors being an actual economist, and the dream they entertain accordingly suspect. (In Ruskin's case, one can't help suspecting that his moral crusade in behalf of the labouring classes may have originated in a buried guilt at having been the pampered child of wealthy parents.) Ransom's contribution, 'Reconstructed but Unregenerate', deplored again and again the acquisitive aspects of modern society, its addiction to 'gross material prosperity.' Again and again he celebrated 'leisure' as the virtue of a community in which a man could 'envelop both his work and his play with a leisure which permitted the activity of intelligence.' Leisure is commended repeatedly, and in the midst of these commendations, Ransom remarks glancingly, 'Slavery was a feature monstrous enough in theory, but, more often than not, humane in practice; and it is impossible to believe that its abolition alone could have effected any great revolution in society.' What *has* effected a great social revolution, in Ransom's view, is the loss of leisure exacted by the pace and goals of industrialism, which, he said, 'enslaves [men] to toil and turnover.' The fact is that in the course of his essay, Ransom uses 'slavery' or one of its cognate forms, metaphorically and reprovingly, a good number of times to refer to the bondage that industrialism entails, but only once literally, in the sentence quoted above, in which its faults are declared to be largely theoretical. Reading this was painful to me, and I still find it unpleasant to think about.

Is it true that your first poem appeared in The Kenyon Review *as a result of a slip on Ransom's part? If this too is dealt with in your essay, please don't worry about quoting from it again; I won't be the only one not to have seen it.*

I did write about this in my essay, and, my memory of the incident being less clear now than it was when I wrote about it, I will do as you advise. Shortly after submitting a poem to the *Review*, 'I went to call upon [Ransom] in his office for some help and advice about a class I was teaching. It had something to do with Shakespeare, as I remember, and we were deeply and vigorously into it, when I looked past his head to the blackboard where he habitually wrote down the names of the contributors to the next issue of the *Review*, in the order in which they would appear. And there, to my astonishment, high on the list, and right between Trilling and Bentley, was my name. At this point, Mr Ransom was being very animated about Macbeth, and all for my benefit, but after a minute or two I could not contain myself, and abandoning all decorum, I interrupted him to ask whether this meant that I was to be in the next issue. He turned around to look at the blackboard, and in his very gentle southern voice said, "I seem to have made a slight mistake," whereupon he rose, went to the blackboard and erased the *H* in front of my name, and put down *Br* instead. The fact is, he did actually publish my poem in the issue following this one; though it seems to me possible that simple embarrassment forced this upon him ... I can't believe he would have been much taken with it. But at this period he was often preoccupied with Freud, and particularly with the essay on Wit and the Unconscious, and such slips could not be regarded as wholly insignificant.'

But if embarrassment had anything to do with your first appearance in the magazine, it could hardly have had anything to do with all your other appearances there. Thirteen of your poems appeared in the Review *between 1947 and 1954.*

I suppose not.

34

Lowell and Jarrell had left Kenyon by the time you arrived, but had you looked at their work?

I only discovered their work after leaving Kenyon. I bought a copy of Lowell's first book, *Land of Unlikeness*, printed in an edition of 250 copies. I read Jarrell as a critic before I got to know his poetry.

When did you encounter Lowell and Jarrell in person?

I met Jarrell only fleetingly once or twice, though we corresponded. He wrote me a very kind and admiring letter about a poem of mine. But I never really knew him. I first met Lowell, then married to Jean Stafford, at around the same time; and John Thompson as well. They were all living in or visiting New York; they were all friends of Robie's, and at that time Robie and I were sharing a cold-water flat on the lower East Side, in New York, while he worked at *Gourmet Magazine*, and I was trying to write a novel, which didn't pan out. I was genuinely awed by these writers who were already established, and celebrities of a sort.

Who else were you taught by while at Kenyon? Am I right in thinking Empson was there at that time?

Empson, whom I revered (and still do) was not at Kenyon when I was a student there, but came at a later time when a summer program called The Kenyon School of English had been established. It brought together some quite extraordinary faculties that included at one time or another, besides Empson, F.O. Matthiessen, Richard Chase, Austin Warren, Eric Bentley, L.C. Knights, Allen Tate, Cleanth Brooks, and others. But when I was a student at Kenyon College, I studied not only with Ransom but with Charles Coffin, who wrote a good book on Donne. And I spent a lot of cheerful, profitable time talking with Philip Blair Rice, who taught Philosophy.

Who else attended those classes, as students?

I've lost track of most of my fellow students who were at Kenyon at the time. One of them, Edwin Watkins, now teaches somewhere in Texas. Another was Oscar Emmett Williams, a 'concrete' poet, also lost in the dark backward and abysm of time. There was a husky young man named Harry Gregg. Kenyon had a rule (which didn't apply to me as a 'special', i.e. non-matriculating, student) that at least half the Sunday chapel services had to be attended, and Harry found, when 'dance weekend' arrived, that he had allowed so many Sundays to lapse that he had no choice but to attend. The difficulty was that, having escorted his date to her residence hall, he found it was early morning; and he was presented with the miserable choice of going to bed for a very few hours, with the danger of not waking in time, or else of trying to stay up for the first service. He elected the latter, and showed up for chapel in rather dishevelled evening dress. He was also stumbling a good deal, and though he seated himself in the rear, was anything but inconspicuous. The chaplain, a very mild-mannered man named Swann, invited any who were inebriated to leave. I don't know whether anyone else left, but Harry stayed. Eventually, when communion was offered, Harry came forward and reverently bit the chaplain's hand.

After your year at Kenyon, you went back to New York, to attend classes at N.Y.U. being given by Allen Tate. How had this come about? And what are your abiding memories of Tate?

I had met Tate at Kenyon during one of those summer sessions. I asked him if I could study with him in New York, again on the G.I. Bill, and he agreed. I used to come once a week to the Greenwich Village apartment he shared with his wife, Caroline Gordon, bringing whatever poems I had written, about which he was very tactful in his comments. He was always gentlemanly, ironic and courteous. He was very kind to me, and when he got a job teaching at Minnesota, and wanted to leave, he recommended me to take over his teaching job at N.Y.U., which I did.

You began teaching at about this time, but I wonder if you could clear up an uncertainty I have about where you were doing this teaching? One source — The Burdens of Formality — has it that you instructed at Bard and N.Y.U., but another — Contemporary Poets — has it that you instructed at Kenyon, Iowa and N.Y.U.

In one way or another, both sources were right. Not counting my undergraduate math teaching at Bard, my first real teaching job was at Kenyon, for one term. From there I went to Iowa, where I was a graduate teaching assistant. In my second term there I had what in those primitive days was called a 'nervous breakdown', and which today would be styled a 'post-traumatic shock syndrome'. It was arrogant and foolish of me to have supposed that my war experiences could be smoothly expunged by a couple of weeks of heavy drinking. I returned to my parents' home in New York and entered psychoanalysis. Of course my analyst, a good and decent man, but an orthodox Freudian, was not prepared to believe that my troubles were due wholly, or even largely, to the war, so we went ambling back together, down the rocky garden path to my infancy. But I think he must have helped me, as much by his kindness and patience as anything else. Anyway, after that I went to N.Y.U., courtesy of Tate, and only in 1952 did I get a full-time teaching job at Bard at a salary of $3,600 a year. As a single man I could live well enough on that. At all these places (except for the brief fling at teaching math) I was teaching either poetry writing or something like freshman English, with, sometimes, a little Renaissance poetry and some Shakespeare thrown in.

Did you enjoy the teaching, or was it a chore?

I enjoyed it enormously. Like many young teachers, I found it easy to establish a rapport with students not much younger than myself. And I was truly ignited by my subject — that is, if it was canonical poetry and literature, as distinguished from the poems written by students. And this continued to be true throughout most of my teaching life. During the final ten years or so before retirement, things changed radically and tragically for the worse. English departments — not mine alone, but many throughout the country — broke up into embattled, intransigent factions demanding exclusive allegiance in behalf of their own mostly ideological agendas: feminism, black studies, gay studies, prison literature, deconstruction, structuralism, disestablishmentarianism, all manner of angry causes that were only marginally related to literature. Whole curricula were devised to justify one or another variety of resentment. This was appealing to quite a few students, who were happy to enlist under the banner of outrage rather than submit themselves to the demanding discipline of careful thought and laborious research. And for the teachers, it clearly meant a good deal in the way of mental relaxation. It was, in some ways, the strange fruit of interdisciplinary studies, which allowed you to know a little bit of some form of inquiry and apply it in an easy selective way to such small provinces of literature as you might be acquainted with. It's my guess that Plato's highly theoretical philosopher-king would, in the practical world, turn out to be both a poor philosopher and a lousy king. I suppose Gibbon would have pointed out Marcus Aurelius and Antoninus Pius as exceptions, but, to return to the point, it seems to me that these days very few who teach at the college and university level are devoted to literature for its own sake, and deeply acquainted with it. Instead, they are pulpit-thumping ideologues, sociologists, reformers. These days it's possible to find long books about the work of some poet in which not a single line of his work is quoted or discussed.

You obtained an M.A. from Columbia in 1950, and the following year won the Prix de Rome fellowship — the first one ever to be awarded for writing. Can you tell us what this meant to you, and how you spent your time in Italy?

The winning of that prize, and the year in Rome to which it entitled me was one of the most satisfactory experiences of my life. My chief competitor for the prize, I was later to discover, was Jack Kerouac. Rome to me was a revelation: exciting, beautiful, full of infinite complexity. One of the great luxuries of a year at the American Academy in Rome was the opportunity to spend that time in the august company of classicists, archaeologists, art and architectural historians, who were brilliantly illuminating to listen to about every aspect of the city, including its best restaurants. I wrote most of my first book of poems while there. But the fact is that I was already in Italy when news of the prize reached me. I was in Ischia. I had gone to Europe in the first place on savings from my discharge from the army, and at the invitation of a friend, also from the army, who was living in a roomy flat in Amsterdam, while paying serious and honourable court to a Dutch girl, whose parents did not disapprove of him, but who were guarded about undue haste. He invited me to share his flat, and when it turned out that the marriage would be delayed even longer than he had supposed, we cast about for a comparatively inexpensive place to settle until all the formalities could be agreed on and arranged. A newspaper ad led us to Ischia, and it was there I met Auden.

What sort of impression did Auden make on you? And what sort of impression did you make on him, do you think?

There was a little expatriate group settled in the town of Porto d'Ischia, where Auden summered. Some of these had been college friends of Chester Kallman, Auden's companion. There were two such American couples, and it was through them that I was introduced to Auden. We were initially shy of one another, for understandable reasons. I'm sure that when he first learned I wrote poetry he must have feared I might impose myself on him. For my part, I was awed by his fame and delighted by his poems, and I also feared that any forwardness on my part might be construed as either intrusive or sexually flirtatious, and I was eager to avoid both impressions. Eventually, we got to know and like one another. He invited me to show him some of my work, and he read and discussed it with great care and sensitivity. At one point he recommended that I change the phrase 'bachelor oyster' to 'celibate oyster' for reasons that must have meant more to him than to me. But he came to trust my views and tastes enough so that when he received from America the manuscripts he had to read through — there must have been nearly a hundred, though triage and elimination had been done State-side — to pick the Yale Younger Poet of the year, he asked me if I would help him read, and we spent a very long, silent afternoon, dividing the stack of manuscripts between us. (It went faster than I had expected, much of the stuff being very bad indeed.) When we finished, neither of us had found a single manuscript of merit. This irritated and surprised him because he knew that at least one poet of talent had entered the competition, and this meant that poet's submission had been eliminated by the helpful winnowers back in the States. Auden decided to write directly to the candidate, and ask that the manuscript be submitted directly to him in Ischia. This was done, and the prize that year went to John Ashbery.

I gather that one of the things Auden complained about in your own work was an 'excess of detail'. What other criticisms can you remember? And how useful were they?

I don't recall his ever complaining about 'excess of detail,' though he might have. It was pretty long ago.

You mentioned it in a letter to Tate, which was written that October. It's in the Tate archive in Princeton.

The complaint of 'excess of detail', by itself and out of context, would mean nothing to me, either as it might have applied to the poems I was writing in those days, or even as a general comment on any poem. After all, attention to detail characterizes some of the poetry I love best, and some that Auden loved as well. Take Hardy, for one. But I would add Elizabeth Bishop and Lowell and Hopkins and Frost. I probably would have left this as a minor enigma had I not before me Edward Mendelson's new study, *Later Auden*, which I think may supply the key to the mystery. Writing of the period when WWII began, Mendelson declares that 'Auden argued to himself that the only acts open to him were private ones of teaching and praise. In his elegy for Yeats he portrayed these acts as the work of an exceptional individual who braved the realm of death and transformed the irrational powers; they were acts achieved through the mysterious power of a poet's gift, and were unconstrained acts that might teach a justice they would never impose.' Mendelson and Auden make much of this idea of the 'gift', which at moments in the text sounds almost as though it were a vocation or a calling, in the religious sense. But it turns out to be partial, that is, fractional: 'Auden mistrusted Yeats as an ally even when he defended him, and knew that in both life and art the gift was not enough. The gift loves vivid particulars and has no interest in ethics or abstractions ... Arnold and Whitman both interested Auden at this time because each was a partial poet – the kind of poet he had left England to avoid becoming. "They represent approaches to life which are eternally hostile, but both necessary, the way of particularizing senses as against the way of the generalizing intellect".' (It is perhaps worth noting that Auden's distinction here is close to one made by Eliot in the third of his Clark Lectures, where he states: 'There are ... essentially two ways in which poetry can add to human experience. One is by perceiving and recording accurately the world – of both sense and feeling – as given at any moment; the other by extending the frontiers of this world. The first is the first in order of generation – you find it in Homer; and I do not say that it is necessarily the second in the order of value. A new and wider and loftier world, such as that into which Dante will introduce you, must be built upon a solid foundation of the old tangible world; it will not descend like Jacob's ladder. Among the poets who have extended reality – and I will admit that they are those who interest me the most – I place Dante first absolutely, and Baudelaire first in recent time.') From the very first, of course, Auden's poetic diction had been full of abstractions: *Love, Time, History, Death, the enemy, terror.* Late in his life I believe he acknowledged that his poor eyesight made him indifferent to many visual experiences. At the same time, he grew up an omnivorous reader of scientific texts as well as philosophy, psychology and history, which sought for patterns, comprehensive views, arrived at through synthesizing methods. I have no doubt that this point of view would quite correctly have found in my poems, both of that time and since, a marked avoidance of abstractions, which Pound warned poets to go in fear of, and which other modernists seemed to avoid.

Did you debate these matters with him at any time?

No, I was much too shy. There were, of course, things we disagreed about. I was much under the spell of Yeats at this period, and Auden took pleasure in saying provoking things by way of taunting me. For example, he said, 'How theatrical to write, "I have walked and prayed for this young child an hour," as though he had consulted his watch to see how long he'd been at it. And the chances are, it would not have been precisely an hour on the dot; and poetry is no good if it is not precise and accurate.' I was too angered to respond to this sensibly, as I could have had I felt less heated. I should have said that poetry, and Yeats's especially, often oscillates between a compressed and an easy, colloquial diction; that by the phrase 'an hour' nothing more was intended than the equivalent of 'a long time', that no one, least of all an anxious father, times his prayers, nor would wish to give the impression of doing so, and Yeats was fastidious about the impression he gave. Auden also tweaked me (and Yeats) by insisting, with regard to Yeats's lines, 'The intellect of man is forced to choose / Perfection of the life, or of the work ...' that this was, in his own frequently invoked dismissive idiom, 'nonsense'. He insisted that perfection was impossible in either. To this, again, I might have replied, though I was unable to at the time, that as regards 'perfection of the work,' there have been many aestheticians and theoreticians who, adopting the mathematics of Pythagoras, have described 'perfect' sculpture and architecture; and that among these would be Vitruvius, and Palladio, Alberti and Michelangelo, to say nothing of Yeats's own poem on the subject, 'The Statues'. And with regard to 'perfection of the life,' while it might seem impossible to Auden, it certainly was aspired to by those whom the church regarded as saints, and this is clearly what Yeats meant. He meant, furthermore, that the two goals were mutually exclusive; and he was by no means the first to have held this doctrine, Shaw and Wilde having declared it themselves at one time or another. But I suspect Auden was simply trying to be provoking, and he may well have been disappointed in my silent refusal to rise to his provocation. If he had been a bit shrewder, he might have trapped me into confessing that Yeats was not wholly free from elementary blunders. I myself, when teaching Yeats, have called the attention of my students to these opening lines from that admirable and lovely poem, 'The Wild Swans at Coole'.

> The trees are in their autumn beauty,
> The woodland paths are dry,
> Under the October twilight the water
> Mirrors a still sky;
> Upon the brimming water among the stones
> Are nine-and-fifty swans.
>
> The nineteenth autumn has come upon me
> Since I first made my count; ...

The problem raised by these lines has to do with the great difficulty in counting large numbers of swans, especially when they're in motion. For they tend infuriatingly to resemble one another, and it is not easy to determine which ones have been counted and to avoid counting any of them twice or even more. I suspect this would be true even for so small a number as twelve or fifteen, to say nothing of fifty-nine.

Europe was a popular destination for American poets in this period. John Ashbery, Richard Howard, Robert Lowell, James Merrill, W.S. Merwin, Adrienne Rich, James Wright — these, and I daresay a number of others, all spent time there. And some, of course, stayed for more than a matter of months: Lowell was there for three years, Ashbery for ten ... What do you think the attraction was? Or is that too general a question?

Ashbery lived in Paris, I saw nothing of him. I saw the Lowells both in Ischia and in Florence, and James Merrill in Rome. Much later in our lives my wife and I ran into the James Wrights in the Arena Chapel in Padua. Merwin I never saw abroad, nor Richard Howard. We probably all went to Europe for different reasons. In my own case, it was first to go back for pleasure after having had to fight a war there (though I had no desire whatever to trace my earlier movements or revisit Germany). And then it was to enjoy the benefits of the fellowship that sent me to Rome. In Merwin's case, his wife had early bought a farm in the south of France, and he had maintained a flat in London that he allowed Ted Hughes and Sylvia Plath to use as an adjunct working studio, apart from the flat in which they lived. Lowell lived for a while in Amsterdam. He was all over the map.

Your first collection appeared in 1954, when you were 31. It took its title, A Summoning of Stones, *from a statement of George Santayana's — 'to call the stones themselves to their ideal places, and enchant the very substance and skeleton of the world' — a statement used by you as an epigraph to the whole book. Your second collection,* The Hard Hours, *appeared thirteen years after that, and there too there was a reference to Santayana, this time in the form of a poem commemorating the philosopher's death, which occurred in 1952. Later still, in your fourth collection,* The Venetian Vespers, *there was yet another reference to be found, in lines which echo a famous statement of his, taken from* The Life of Reason: *'Those who will not be taught by history / Have as their curse the office to repeat it ...' Santayana's writings had obviously made quite an impression on you ...*

I know he is not much thought of nowadays in philosophic circles. But I was deeply impressed by the style, the agility of his prose, which was elegantly hieratic, and if not quite dandified, then at least aristocratically Spanish and grandee. He wrote with a delicate and humane irony that pleased me, though there were times when I disagreed with him profoundly. His kind of discourse is not much cherished by the most influential philosophic voices of today, which, for that matter, speak mostly in French.

I know that Lowell visited Santayana while he was in Rome, but did you visit him too? Some of the details in the first stanza of the poem I just mentioned might suggest that you had been to the convent where he was being nursed. Or were these simply imagined?

I never met Santayana, and my poem about him was completely imagined, though I may quite possibly have seen a photograph of a loggia or cloister in that convent where he stayed.

You once described A Summoning of Stones *as the work of an 'advanced apprentice'. This must have been a judgement on the book taken as a whole — half of whose contents you ended up suppressing — not a judgement on all thirty of the poems? Because poems like 'La Condition Botanique', 'The Gardens of the Villa d'Este', and 'Japan' — my favourites, I have to say — seem to me to be the work of someone who's found his own voice, not the work of someone who's still employing others'. Or do you disagree?*

This is a difficult question, about which I may not be objective. I believe that when I made the dismissive remark I meant that the general tone of the book, taken as a whole, was jaunty and distant, cool and artificed, and I still think this is true. I knew perfectly well at the time that I wasn't able to do justice to some of the horrors of existence I had reason to know about. This is not to say that I am not modestly proud of the 'Villa D'Este' and 'Botanique', but that in writing them I was enjoying the challenge of writing 'essay poems', wandering discourse that could lead anywhere and stop when it pleased. This was some of Auden's influence. And the more serious poems, 'Japan', 'A Deep Breath at Dawn' (much Yeats in that one), 'A Roman Holiday' (much early Lowell in that one), 'Christmas is Coming', all put the terror of reality at an artistic distance, and were too full of 'devices'.

Can you give an example or two?

The lines in 'A Deep Breath' about admiring a distant view through the shell-penetrated body of a dead soldier who returns as a ghost is too fanciful and unreal, and almost embarrassing. Though not because it involves ghosts. Hardy and Yeats and Eliot all wrote about them well enough. And in 'Christmas is Coming' the war has been curiously sanitized by being treated as an allegory. The poem is a kind of bad dream, with nursery rhyme refrains meant to sound ominous. The poem floats in some region between raw fact, dream, and parable, in what, in the end, seems to me a soft and impalpable blur. Allen Tate, when I showed the poem to him in draft, asked, 'Who are the poor?' I don't know what he meant by the question, whether he was inquiring into my knowledge of a class to which I could not claim to belong, whether I was 'affecting' to be one of the unemployed, or whatever. When I answered quite innocently, 'Why, we all are,' he was utterly silent and without comment. And the sense that I was writing (among other things) a universal allegory is something that to me gravely weakens the poem.

In writing those poems I felt I was performing duties that pulled me in opposing directions: one was to honour and commemorate the tragedies and horror of war, while the other was to compose elegant and well-crafted poems in the manner of those poets who were still my models.

Can you tell me how you hit on the similar stanza forms of 'La Condition Botanique' and 'The Gardens of the Villa d'Este'?

First of all, as I said, I wanted to write free-flowing essay poems, and a stanza that expands in the middle provides a kind of leeway for improvisation and digression. That is part of the answer. Without perfect confidence I can add that I was familiar with Dylan Thomas's 'Vision and Prayer', in which he uses diamond-shaped stanzas, and I also knew George Herbert's 'Aaron', which again enlarges and diminishes in the course of its stanzas. It's hard for me to guess how much Thomas or Herbert played a conscious part in my design, but I do know that the attempt to duplicate the forms established by other poets is a challenge and incentive that has been valuable to not a few poets. For example, when Lowell moved in on Tate in Tennessee, they seem to have challenged one another to compose a poem in the form of Michael Drayton's 'To the Virginian Voyage'. Out of that rivalry came Tate's 'Ode to Our Young Pro-consuls of the Air', and Lowell's poem, published in *Land of Unlikeness*, called 'Satan's Confession'.

What critical reception was A Summoning of Stones *given?*

I dimly remember that it got some nice reviews, one in *The New Yorker* by Louise Bogan. But it was remaindered before even half the printing was sold. These days, rare book dealers tell me that a copy goes for about $200.

After your return from Italy, and up to the point at which you published your first collection, you'd been instructing at Bard, where I believe one of your colleagues was Saul Bellow. Did you get to know each other?

Yes, I greatly admired and liked Saul. He is a wonderful man, extraordinarily charming, witty, good-humoured, cultivated and widely-read. He seemed to have an enormous fund of jokes — mostly ethnic, Jewish jokes — on call for any situation. And without ostentation, he larded his conversation with tags of poetry, some of it quite recondite. He was good company, and a generous man.

Another of your colleagues was Heinrich Blücher, and I assume you must have got to know him and his wife, Hannah Arendt, since 'More Light! More Light!' is dedicated to them?

Yes, I knew Heinrich and Hannah. Heinrich taught at Bard for some years, giving a course required of all freshmen, and called 'The Common Course'. I taught a section of it myself for a number of years, and grew very close to Heinrich, who used to get a lift from me as I drove to and from Bard, both of us residing in New York. It was a 'great ideas' course, involving more or less canonical texts from Plato, Buddha, Heraclitus, the Bible, Homer, and much else I can no longer recall. I found myself uncomfortable with some of Heinrich's ideas about these texts, but I found the man himself exceptionally endearing. He would visit me every evening for a drink (most commonly a 'bullshot', which is about four parts beef bouillon to one of vodka) and then we would meet friends at a local dive for dinner.

Blücher was the model for Gottfried Rosenbaum in Jarrell's Pictures from an Institution, a figure who delights as much by the quirkiness of his heavily accented English as by his learning, his taste, his good humour. How accurate a portrayal was this?

Heinrich's command of English was far from idiomatic, and sometimes it *was* inadvertently amusing. When pleased to be done with some unpleasant task, he would remark that it was well to have this 'in the behind'. And, in an amusing allusion to Swift's Yahoo, he would dismiss someone of inferior qualities as a 'regular Yoohoo'. Hannah, so far as I can recall, was never given to such lapses. She spoke wonderfully well, though she too had a pronounced German accent.

How well did you get to know her?

Hannah entertained me a number of times at their New York apartment, partly in thanks for my chauffeur services to Heinrich, but also out of her generous hospitality, and once took me out to a good French restaurant which specialized in cassoulet. She and I met in sorrow at a memorial service for Auden, held at the cathedral of St. John the Divine. I was to take part in the service by reading a poem of Auden's – I don't remember which one – as were a number of others, including Robert Penn Warren, Galway Kinnell, Muriel Rukeyser, Richard Wilbur, William Meredith, Richard Howard and Ursula Niebuhr. I didn't know when we commiserated with one another that evening that Auden had once proposed marriage to Hannah. It was clear, however, that she was deeply grieved. I had enormous regard for her; her learning was almost limitless, or so it seemed to me, and not least because it commanded regions of scholarship wholly unknown to me. She was also a woman of considerable charm.

Do you remember when you first met her? Was it at Bard?

No, Hannah rarely visited Bard, though she and Heinrich are buried in the small college cemetery side by side. No, it was at a birthday party for Auden, a party which he himself was unable to attend for some reason. Unlike Auden's usual birthday parties, it was a decorous event, because it was held at the home of Reinhold and Ursula Niebuhr.

Heinrich made me a good number of gifts of books, including the complete works of Shakespeare in the Schlegel translation (printed, infuriatingly, in old gothic type, which I could only barely decipher). At the end of our association, we were very close, and I felt the deepest affection for him. I was one of the very few people present (the others were Reamer Kline, the President of Bard, Irma Brandeis and, of course, Hannah) when, in a private ceremony in their apartment, Heinrich was given an honorary degree by Bard, something which meant a great deal to him since, for some reason, he had no earned degree.

1954 was quite a big year for you. You published your first collection, you won your first Guggenheim award, and you got married. Was it the

Guggenheim that enabled you to give up instructing at Bard, not to resume teaching until you went to Smith, in 1956?

Yes, a Guggenheim allowed me to return to Rome for a year at the American Academy once more, where Richard Wilbur was also in residence.

Wilbur had already published The Beautiful Changes *and* Ceremony *by that time. Did you know his work well?*

Yes, I think I did. But the curious fact is that I own no copy of the first of his books, and my copy of the second is dated September, 1960. In those youthful days, knowledge of the work of new poets was something to be acquired, as it were, monthly, or at least quarterly. Everyone, myself included, read the leading 'little magazines', some of them very élite, and we came upon the newest and latest poems one by one as they appeared in the best and the most avant-garde of those journals. I knew Wilbur's poems of that time entirely by their isolated periodical publications. I was an avid reader of all the earliest and most advanced of those journals, including *transition, Hound and Horn*, and Cyril Connolly's *Horizon*, and it was in the last of these that I, an American, discovered the work of Eudora Welty. As for Wilbur's work, I must have known it from *The New Yorker*, among other places, and from anthologies, such as Oscar Williams's *Little Treasury of American* or *Modern Poetry* series. Wilbur and I had actually met at a rooftop cocktail party given by Williams in downtown Manhattan.

How did you get the job at Smith College, and what did it involve?

Let me answer the second part of your question first. I taught freshman English at Smith, and nothing else the entire time (three years) I was there. Freshman English consisted of analytical study of short-stories, a novel, and a good deal of lyric poetry. The authors we read included Henry James, D.H. Lawrence, Conrad, Chekhov, and the more or less usual catalogue of poets. Among my students was one who, by a kind of miracle, and many years later, would become my second wife. As for how I got the job, the simple truth is that I don't remember. I suspect that what I did was what most job candidates did in those remote and simple days: I sent off applications and vitae to any place that seemed likely, either because they advertised a vacancy or because rumour (which was abundant, there being many academics in Rome and at the American Academy) led me in that direction.

Did you get to know Sylvia Plath and Ted Hughes while you were at Smith?

Yes. Sylvia was a colleague of mine at Smith College. I liked them both very much, but this was a particularly troubled and unhappy period of my life. During my three years there two sons were born, one of them during my first year. His mother got breast fever immediately after the birth, and could not nurse him, or, for that matter, do anything whatever. Consequently, I did all the shopping for food, all the cooking for my wife and myself, all the laundry, including the diapers (there were no disposable ones then), and there was no clothes-drier where we lived so that all the laundry had to be hung on lines and taken down when dry. Moreover, there was the formula for the baby to make, and all the night feedings to give, and during this time I was teaching full time. The chairman of the English department in those days, a rather self-absorbed, near-sighted martinet, upbraided me for not providing enough written comment on the papers I returned to my students. I was too dumbfounded to explain my predicament, which he should have been fully aware of in the first place, since other faculty were. In her journals, Sylvia also expressed a bewildered irritation at the fact that my wife and I never returned the hospitality she showed us. This was because my wife simply refused to entertain — in part, at least, because she couldn't cook, and was embarrassed about it. Immediately after our second son was born she went ice-skating and broke her leg, so I had to go through the whole routine — cooking, shopping, laundry, formulas, night-feedings — all over again, and, of course, while teaching full-time as before. Still, there were a few good people at Smith while I was there, beginning with Ted and Sylvia. There was also Daniel Aaron, who became a friend later on. There was Newton Arvin, a gentle and brilliant man, and a critic of the first order, now seriously undervalued. There was Helen Bacon, a gifted classicist, with whom I was later to collaborate on a translation of Aeschylus. And of all of them, the one most dear to me, Elizabeth Drew, an English woman who wrote on modern poetry, was a friend of Auden's, and the soul of kindness. She was fully aware of my marital plight, so there was no reason why the fidgety chairman should not have been as well. Anyway, Smith contrived profoundly to offend Ted and Sylvia in a manner that made them decide to leave after a single year. Sylvia was teaching the same courses as I, and Ted stayed at home, writing, keeping house, but fretful, with too much time on his hands. He wanted to teach too, and

Sylvia arranged a meeting for him with the chairman. Ted was told they couldn't hire him because he had no teaching experience, though this had been no barrier to their having appointed Sylvia, who had none either. But of course she was a Smith graduate. The indignation Sylvia felt about this, and which Ted probably felt as well, though he kept his feelings under better control than she, was little short of explosive. They firmly resolved to leave at the end of the year, and they did so, to the utter astonishment of the chairman, who hadn't the slightest clue he had offended them. They settled for a year or so in Boston, where Sylvia joined Anne Sexton and George Starbuck in one of Lowell's classes at Boston University.

Your teaching at Smith came to an end in 1959, the year you won your second Guggenheim. It was also the year in which you and your wife separated, taking your two boys with her. How did all these developments affect you? Are you the sort of person who can go on writing in the midst of great turmoil, or are you the sort who, as Kafka might have put it, needs both hands to ward off the blows?

When I'm troubled or unhappy my faculties are paralyzed and I can't write at all. And, alas, I was unhappy virtually throughout my first marriage, which lasted five-and-a-half years, to be followed by my total separation from my children. The divorce decree required her to live within a certain distance from New York City, so that I could continue to see them regularly. But in due course she found herself engaged to a very wealthy young Belgian, and she told me, 'Of course, you have a legal right to make me stay here; but if you do, I will be very unhappy, and if I'm unhappy, the children will be, too.' Against such an argument I was quite powerless.

Maybe I can quote from an earlier passage in Kafka's diaries than the one I was alluding to just now, only I'd like to hear your reaction to what he says there:

> *'Have never understood how it is possible for almost everyone who writes to objectify his sufferings in the very midst of undergoing them; thus I, for example, in the midst of my unhappiness, in all likelihood with my head still smarting from unhappiness, sit down and write to someone: I am unhappy. Yes, I can even go beyond that and with as many flourishes as I have the talent for, all of which seem to have*

nothing to do with my unhappiness, ring simple, or contra-
puntal, or a whole orchestration of changes on my theme.
And it is not a lie, and it does not still my pain; it is simply a
merciful surplus of strength at a moment when suffering has
raked me to the bottom of my being and plainly exhausted
all my strength. But then what kind of surplus is it?'

I fear that I have never been granted Kafka's bountiful surplus of energy
that he was able to call up during crises or depressions. I can think of few
things more enviable. I have no reserves of imaginative energy to draw
on in periods of darkness. Ransom, who proposed what might be thought
of as a doctrine of 'aesthetic distance', which I found easy to adopt, used
to say that the poet who wanted to write a love poem would be well
advised not to do so in the first fine frenzy of his passion. He would be
too close to his experience, too giddy with its pleasing chaos and turbu-
lence to be able even to understand himself, let alone to put his feelings
and thoughts into some disciplined order. The writer, Ransom would
maintain, who can best create powerful feelings in his reader is precisely
the one who has mastered these feelings before trying to set them down
on paper. And Eliot would add to this that the writer can also describe
and evoke experiences he's never actually had — a matter that the
stunning variety of Shakespeare's and Dickens's and Browning's charac-
ters ought unarguably to demonstrate, though the tendency in our era is
to regard lyric poems as purely the seismography of the life of the
individual soul. Flaubert wrote to his mother in December, 1850, ex-
pressing much the same requirement of absolute personal detachment
that Ransom recommends, though in Flaubert's case, far more severely,
and by way of explaining that he was determined never to marry, feeling
that his vocation as a writer forbade it. He wrote, 'You can depict wine,
love, and women on the condition that you are not a drunkard, a lover, or
a husband.'

That reminds me of something Pascal once said: 'Few men speak hum-
bly of humility, chastely of chastity, sceptically of scepticism.'

How very sound; and how chastening.

After the departure of your children for Europe, you had to be hospital-
ized for depression. How long did that last, and what longer-term effects,
if any, did it have on your life and career?

Deep breath. I was hospitalized for about three months. I was put on

Thorazine, and some other medications I no longer can name. These were alternative treatments to the electric shock therapy more commonly administered at that hospital, which was called Gracey Square. (There were public pay phones in the corridor on my floor, and outsiders could call in through those phones, which could be answered by any patient, and it was more or less standard practice for patients to pick up the phone and say, cheerfully, 'Crazy Square.') I met some nice people there, and some that were deeply, frighteningly troubled. (One, who had to be subdued with a hypodermic, makes his way briefly into a poem of mine.) I myself was merely badly depressed. I was fortunate in liking and trusting my doctor, who, wisely, had forbidden, with my complete consent, any attempt on the part of my parents to visit me — a prohibition my father took pains to violate. I don't know how he got in, but he did, on the pretext of bringing me some toothpaste or cigarettes. He suddenly appeared one day, very briefly, in the hall, and handed me these things. And his grin was terrible, almost triumphant. I was revolted. We exchanged no words. It was after I was released that Lowell went out of his way to be kind, helpful and friendly to me. He was especially gentle and considerate, knowing well what such institutions are like, though we did not discuss the topic. Frederick Morgan, the editor of *The Hudson Review* was also uncommonly kind to me during this period. Fred and his co-editor, Joseph Bennett, had given me, just around the time my wife and I had separated, a *Hudson Review* Fellowship, meant to free me to write. I told Fred candidly that I was not going to be able to use it, and that he would be wise to offer it to someone else. But he refused to reconsider, and the consequence of this was that when my wife departed, she quite literally cleaned me out, taking with her, among other things, my baby grand (though she couldn't play a note), a painting that had belonged to my grandfather, and all but five hundred dollars in our joint bank account, including, of course, the Hudson grant. As to 'long-term effects,' it seems to me that if it can be said that everyone has some overriding fear, mine has been insanity. And I think this lurks behind a number of my poems.

You told J.D. McClatchy that you had a theory about why it was that so many American poets had been affected by mental illness, but you declined to set it out, on the grounds that there wouldn't be enough space. If I promise to make the space, can I induce you to say something about your theory?

That's a tall order, and you wouldn't have nearly enough space. It's a book-length topic. And it applies not simply to Americans but to poets of,

I suspect, all western nations. I once sketched a preliminary list of poets who were mentally unstable or who committed suicide. In America alone this included Hart Crane, Ted Roethke, Lowell, Sexton, Plath, James Wright, Berryman, Elizabeth Bishop, Hayden Carruth, Eliot, Pound, Jarrell, Mona Van Duyn ... There must be many I've forgotten.

I can only think of one: Delmore Schwartz.

But Europe would contribute its share: Trakl, Paul Celan, Hölderlin, John Clare, Cowper, Gérard de Nerval, Christopher Smart, Baudelaire, Swift, Sergéy Esénin, Mayakóvsky and Tsvetáeva (both of whom committed suicide) and Nietzsche. Blake claimed he had been granted interviews with angels, and used to sit around in the buff outdoors with his wife. Dr. Johnson feared insanity most of his life and forced himself to undertake arithmetical computations to maintain his sanity. Mrs. Thrale once found him 'taking the national debt, computing it at 180 millions sterling, and then calculating whether it "would, if converted into silver, serve to make a meridian of that metal, I forget how broad, for the globe of the whole world."' Byron took up the study of Armenian for much the same therapeutic reasons. Wordsworth recognized the danger in 'Resolution and Independence', Shelley did the same in 'Julian and Maddalo', Thomas Gray was apprehensive, and so was Tennyson. I'm sure that many have slipped my mind at the moment.

Well, there was Donne, of course, who confessed that he had a 'sickely inclination' to suicide. And later on there was William Collins (who, like Clare and Smart, spent time in the madhouse), Chatterton (who took arsenic and died at the age of 18), and Hopkins (whose Dark Sonnets were written during a period of deep depression).

As to the cause, I should declare right at the start that I profoundly distrust sociological diagnoses and easy historical generalizations. One can only point to the curious appearance of poets (and other artists as well) roughly at the start of the eighteenth century, who were either certifiably mad, suicidal, drug addicts, or all three. 'Alienated', 'poète maudit', became familiar descriptive terms. Beginning at least with Blake's declaration, 'The road of excess leads to the palace of wisdom,' which not only sounds like vintage Oscar Wilde but seemed dedicated to undermining conventional society and received religion, the profession of poetry came to be associated in the public's mind with the nut house, the loony bin. Even that retiring lady of Amherst would declare, 'Much madness is divinest sense,' which is either respectable Platonism or the subversion of all social values and civilized discourse. The symptoms seemed to be considered in such works as Nietzsche's 'The Significance of Madness in the History of Morality', and in Foucault's *Madness and Civilization*. The former went mad himself, the latter begins his diagnostic study squarely in the eighteenth century. This doesn't mean that there had never been any crazy poets before. Tasso comes immediately to mind, and in his diary entry for April 21, 1657, John Evelyn noted, '... at my returne step'd into Bedlame, where I saw nothing extraordinary, besides some miserable poore Creatures in chaines, one was mad with making verses ...' Nevertheless, they were more the exception in earlier times. What changed things had something obscurely to do with the status and financial security that pertained to the poet's place in society. Roughly speaking, before the change, poets had either been gentlemen who, as literary dilettantes, wrote for the pleasure and amusement of their friends, and without much care about publication; or else they composed in behalf of and homage to some patron, who would supply their most pressing needs. But the patronage system collapsed, so that writers (including poets) had to make their way in the world of print through commercial publishing and the approval, no longer of individual patrons, but of a public taste that was often capricious and frequently untrained and ill-educated. And, as the public taste showed a decided preference for a good yarn, the novel prospered, newspapers came into their own, and poets found themselves addressing smaller and smaller audiences, composed mainly of their fellow-poets, who regarded them as rivals for the pitifully small notice afforded to poetry.

There are many kinds of evidence testifying to the increasingly marginal role assigned by society to writers of all sorts. By the mid-nineteenth century, literary bohemia was already regarded as laughable. There's an amusing passage in William Gaunt's book, *The Aesthetic Adventure*, dealing with France during the beginning of the Second Empire under Napoleon III. 'By a series of republican (and even Bohemian) revolutions, assisted this is to say by "vagabonds, disbanded soldiers, discharged prisoners, fugitives from the galleys, sharpers, jugglers, professional beggars, pickpockets, conjurors, gamesters, pimps, brothel keepers, porters, men of letters, organ grinders, rag pickers, knife grinders and tinkers," Charles Louis Napoleon, third son of the King of Holland, made himself Emperor of the French. The description of his helpers is that of Karl Marx who, it will be seen, places "men of letters" somewhere between porters and organ grinders; who further described French Bohemia as "the scum, offal, and detritus of society."'

The only people these days who freely speak of their 'inspiration', and use that very word without embarrassment, are fashion designers and hair stylists. No, I'm wrong. One would have to add a lot of people in Holly-wood. Some years ago, Congress, which can hardly resist the chance to get celebrities to testify before its committees, invited some film stars to express their views about the colourization of early black-and-white films, as well as the enhancement of colour in films made before technology in the field had been perfected. A burning issue for all citizens. Almost to a man and woman, these actors were absolute, uncompromising purists. After his congressional appearance, Burt Lancaster offered his views to television reporters, declaring, with a straight face, that the film stars of today were the Michelangelos and Leonardos, the Beethovens and Mozarts of our time. No wonder Eliot said to Empson that 'poetry is a mug's game.' A lot more calls for mention about how poets, driven by desperation, ended up in the garrets where Leoncavallo found them in *La Bohème*, or at the barricades of numberless revolutionary movements. I'm not really qualified to go into this very much further, though it may be that the posture of defiance conducts the poet frequently into the camp of irra-tionality, or at least that the public believes this and wants it this way. Clearly the imputation of singularly refined faculties, imaginative sub-tlety, mental acuity that set Sherlock Holmes apart gave his creator the license to make him an opium addict as well. And Holmes, remember, was independently wealthy, as only a few poets have been. It must in any case be said that to devote your life to doing something that is very diffi-cult and demanding, and that is almost universally disesteemed, can take a heavy toll sooner or later.

I wonder if any solid work has been done on the incidence of instability in poets. A few years ago, I read a book by Anthony Storr according to which surveys done at the University of Iowa's Writers' Workshop found that almost 70% of the writers interviewed had suffered from affective illness of one kind or another, compared with something closer to 10% in the case of the controls. That seemed unbelievably high. Then, more recently, I read the introduction to Ian Hamilton's Oxford Companion to 20th-Century Poetry, where it is said that, of the 1,500 poets listed, 'Twenty-seven had nervous breakdowns, fifteen committed suicide, and fifteen were/are diagnosed as alcoholic.' Assuming no overlap, that worked out to a little under 4%, which seemed remarkably low ...

I guess things must be pretty tough in Iowa; though as far as my own experience goes, the poets I associate with that place are relatively sound: Donald Justice, Jorie Graham, Marvin Bell. As to Mr Hamilton's figures, we might conjecture that he counts only those poets whose entries in the

Companion actually make mention of such problems. Many an outline of a poet's career is reported in that book without taking any note whatever of psychological trouble experienced by the poet.

I asked Ian about this just recently, and you're quite right: he did base his figures on the entries alone.

In which case, James Wright wasn't taken into account. Neither was Jane Kenyon. Neither was Joseph Brodsky (who was committed to a Soviet insane asylum, purely a political action, but on the record none the less.) And neither, for that matter, was I.

By the time your second collection appeared, in 1968, you'd done several more years' teaching at Bard, and were at the end of your first year as a Professor at Rochester. You'd also received a number of other awards, amongst them the Hudson Review Fellowship you mentioned a moment ago, two Ford Fellowships, a Brandeis University Creative Arts Award and a Rockefeller Fellowship. The Hard Hours *itself added two more honours to your already impressive list: the Pulitzer Prize for 1968 and the Loines Award. The acclaim must have been very welcome, but can I ask you: did it exact any kind of cost?*

The acclaim got me a promotion to a named chair, 'The John H. Deane Professor of Poetry and Rhetoric', at the university. (The rhetoric part meant that I was to fall heir to the position of university orator, and expected to compose and read aloud the citations for the recipients of honorary degrees at commencement ceremonies.) And I got a lot of kind mail from friends; Anne Sexton, who had won the prize the year before, wrote jocularly to say 'It's about time.' My publishers were delighted and took me to a fine dinner with some friends of mine in New York. All that part of it was very nice. I also got misquoted in the Rochester papers, which taught me that all too often reporters would rather have you say what they would like you to say instead of what you've really said. And what they would like you to say tends often enough to tax the limits of literacy, though I suppose it's what they think their readers want to read. The Pulitzer Prize is regarded as a big deal in America, largely because it attracts so much notice (and thus sells books) and the notice is conferred because the prize is awarded under the auspices of the School of Journalism of Columbia University, and most of the winners are newspapers and those who write, photograph and draw for them. The papers are not shy about promoting their own triumphs, and willing to share some small portion of the spotlight with a solitary novelist, poet, and dramatist. It doesn't take long, however, for a poet to learn how fleeting is worldly fame. There's a gifted newspaper comic strip artist named Wiley Miller, whose work I often admired, and who ran one strip that concerned a conversation between a father and his something-like-six-year-old son. The father is holding a book he has just purchased at a book-signing event, and says, 'Look ... I was in the bookstore today, and a famous poet was signing his book,' as he holds up an inscribed copy. Child: 'I didn't know you read poetry.' Father: 'Uh .. I don't.' Child: 'Do you know anyone who reads poetry?' Father: 'Ummm .. No.' Child: 'So how does that make him famous to you?' Father: 'Well ... He won a Pulitzer.' A panel follows representing an embarrassed smile on the father, and a bewildered expression on the child; total silence. Father, to the departing child: 'Where are you going?' Child: 'Acting class. I need to brush up on feigning to be impressed.' Father, angrily flourishing the book: 'That's a rather poor attitude toward your future heirloom, mister!!' Child: 'Oh, great. More acting lessons.'

The Hard Hours *opens with 'The Hill', a monologue, whose speaker tells of an experience he'd had while walking through the Piazza Farnese in Rome. One minute it had been sunny and warm, crowded and noisy, the next:*

> *... the noises suddenly stopped,*
> *And it got darker; pushcarts and people dissolved*
> *And even the great Farnese Palace itself*
> *Was gone, for all its marble; in its place*
> *Was a hill, mole-coloured and bare. It was very cold,*
> *Close to freezing, with a promise of snow.*
> *The trees were like old ironwork gathered for scrap*
> *Outside a factory wall. There was no wind,*
> *And the only sound for a while was the little click*
> *Of ice as it broke in the mud under my feet.*
> *I saw a piece of ribbon snagged on a hedge,*
> *But no other sign of life. And then I heard*
> *What seemed the crack of a rifle. A hunter, I guessed;*
> *At least I was not alone. But just after that*
> *Came the soft and papery crash*
> *Of a great branch somewhere unseen falling to earth*
> *And that was all, except for the cold and silence*
> *That promised to last forever, like the hill.*

The speaker claims not have been bothered by this incident in the ten years since it occurred. What moves him to talk about it now is the sudden remembrance of where he'd first encountered that hill:

> *... it lies just to the left*
> *Of the road north of Poughkeepsie; and as a boy*
> *I stood before it for hours in wintertime.*

So, perhaps, one part of the mystery is removed. What had overtaken him in the Piazza wasn't something requiring supernatural explanation, but something permitting explanation in terms of accepted psychological categories — memories, hallucinations, and the like. But if one part of the mystery is removed, another, more serious, remains. Why would a boy stand for hours in front of a scene whose plain bitterness was to leave an adult scared for days?

I wonder if I can ask where that image of the hill comes from? It clearly has some special significance for you, since it, or things very like it, appear in a number of your poems — 'Christmas is Coming', 'The Short End', 'Auspices', 'The Venetian Vespers', 'See Naples and Die', 'Death the Whore' ....

My therapist had a lot of theories about that poem. Anyway, when you ask, 'why would a boy stand for hours in front of a scene of great bitterness?' the answer is, of course, that he does not do so willingly; he is compelled to. And he is compelled to because no one comes to take him away from all this barrenness. You are perfectly right to see arid and defeated landscapes cropping up in a good number of my poems, as is the case with certain winter scenes of Breughel. They were for me a means to express a desolation of the soul. There are such scenes in Hardy, as well as in a fine young poet, not yet well known, named Timothy Murphy. May I quote a short poem of his?

Twice Cursed

> Bristling with fallen trees
> and choked with broken ice
> the river threatens the house.
> I'll wind up planting rice
> if the spring rains don't cease.
> What ancestral curse
> prompts me to farm and worse,
> convert my woes to verse?

I'm not a farmer, and thus not subject to their special dangers, but for me a bleak and forlorn landscape can assemble and convey a deep sense of despair.

'The Hill' serves as a kind of warning to readers of The Hard Hours, *because, as they read their way through the book, they are going to be confronted with visions of plain bitterness, visions of suffering, madness, and death whose power to scare is not in the least mysterious. In one poem we are given vivid descriptions of the daily flogging, and eventual flaying, of the Roman emperor Valerian; in another, a promise is made to the ghost of a child lost to its parents as a result of miscarriage; in a third, the burning at the stake of one Christian by others is juxtaposed with an atrocity committed in the vicinity of Buchenwald ...*

But there are mysteries associated with these poems, and I can get at the most perplexing of them by quoting Flaubert, who wrote to Amélie Bousquet as follows: 'Human life is a sad show, undoubtedly: ugly, heavy and complex. Art has no other end, for people of feeling, than to conjure away the burden and the bitterness.' Is this too narrow a conception of art? Or is there a sense in which your poems can be said to conjure away the burden and bitterness, even as they force us to confront them? I'm the more intrigued by your answer because of what you say in 'Rites and Ceremonies': 'The contemplation of horror is not edifying, / Neither does it strengthen the soul.'

A difficult question to which there is no easy answer. One mistaken way of construing the Flaubert assertion would be to say that he is recommending escape literature and fairy tales that end with the protagonists living happily ever after. But 'conjuring the burden and bitterness away' demands serious necromancy. I would summon to my aid Hardy's apology from 'In Tenebris': 'If a way to the Better there be, it exacts a full look at the Worst.' In his poem called 'No Possum, No Sop, No Taters', Wallace Stevens writes, 'It is here, in this bad, that we reach / The last purity of the knowledge of good.' And I would enlist the further support of Keats in the letter to his brothers in which he says that 'the excellence of every Art is its intensity, capable of making all disagreeables evaporate, from their being in close relationship with Beauty & Truth — Examine King Lear & you will find this examplified [sic] throughout' (21-27 December 1817). The fact is that *Lear* was for many years my favourite among the tragedies, and has never lost its appeal for me. And it has its full component of bleak landscapes. I taught it for years before I found out that there are two proper versions and that I would have to choose between them. I had so grown used and devoted to the conflated text that I found myself unwilling to relinquish some of the lines I prized. Anyway, I've always been on guard, as a reader first of all, against what has been called 'Land-of-heart's-desire' poetry, which tends to be vapid and sentimental. On the other hand, I would still continue to affirm what I wrote about the contemplation of horror not being edifying. I have always found that the stories and paintings of Christian martyrdom are very strange because they can be understood in two different and opposing ways. The orthodox way is to say that they inspire admiration for fixity of faith in the face of the most horrible and obstinate persecution. At the same time, of course, they are often remarkable for their morbidity, and, alas, a part of their meaning seems to concern the ineradicable savagery of the human race; and not just of pagans and infidels but people of all kinds, as the many religious wars among Christians — the Thirty Years' War, the so-called Wars of Religion in Spain, France and the Netherlands being merely examples — have abundantly demonstrated. There's a Byzantine mosaic icon in Washington of 'The Forty Martyrs of Sebaste' — they were 'stripped naked, herded onto a frozen pond, and kept there; to help break down their resistance a fire was kindled and warm baths prepared where they could see them. By the next day most of them were dead; those who were not were killed,' says a little handbook of hagiography. But this is no more than a puny prologue to the Holocaust. It is the Vatican's dubious position that German anti-Semitism as it was exhibited under the Nazis 'had its roots outside Christianity,' and that the people who ran the camps were essentially pagan. This, however, fails to agree with the Nazis' own view of the matter. In Peter Matheson's documentary account, *The Third Reich and the Christian Churches*, he writes of a report by one Hanns Kerrl on the membership and finances of the Churches, dated 3, July, 1944 (not long, that is, before the war ended) — a report sent to Goebbels 'on the request of the Ministry for popular Enlightenment and Propaganda,' containing statistics 'with the rather anxious request that caution be used in their exploitation for propaganda purposes. It is worth noting how little success the National Socialists had in winning people away from their adherence to Christian beliefs. Only 3.5% acknowledged themselves as "Gottgläubige",' a word that Cassell's German dictionary defines as 'followers of the modern German cult of non-Christian theism,' and which Matheson calls simply 'neo-pagans.'

In Philip Larkin's 'Ambulances', passers-by, looking on as people in extremity are fetched off to hospital, are said to 'sense the solving emptiness / That lies just under all we do, / and for a second get it whole, / So

59

permanent and blank and true.' Larkin was clearly no stranger to the
experience he describes here, but my guess is that you are. It's hell you
worry about, not the void ...

I agree. Larkin did not have to serve in the war and he was not a Jew, and
he counted himself lucky on both scores. It may be that one of the ap-
peals of his poetry for many readers lies in his contemplation of 'the solv-
ing emptiness,' which is obscurely comforting. Not paradise, to be sure,
but a kind of beneficent anaesthesia.

Heart's Needle and Life Studies had made a huge impact on the literary
scene in 1960, but the confessional genre they inaugurated seems to
have made little impression on you. Was this simply a question of tem-
perament, or did you have objections to that way of writing, as a number
of other people did?

I had, and have, no objections in principle, and I greatly admire both
Snodgrass and Lowell. But there were a number of poets who came more
and more to exploit the sensational aspects of their lives, and in turn
came to feel that the more sensational their lives were the better, at least
for their careers as poets. Peter Quennell, in writing about Byron, may
have located a source for this attitude. He cites opinions of Byron's, and
writes, 'Verse, he said, was the "lava of the imagination" — its canaliza-
tion into literature prevented its overflow — and, elsewhere, that it was
"the dream of his sleeping passions," the direct image of some experi-
ence he had actually lived through. The poet, in fact, above all things,
must be a Personality! Few personalities have more than a pathological
interest; and it is to Byron's personal influence on modern literature that
we owe the whole tribe of gifted exhibitionists, ranging in scope from
Alfred de Musset to Dowson, who have attempted to "live" their poems
as well as write them.' There have been plenty, of course, to follow after
de Musset and Dowson. One cannot fail to be struck, however, at how
diametrically opposed is this view to that of Keats, who said the poet had
no personality of his own, no identity. In any case, this sort of thing is not
for me. I have in fact tried to disguise myself in my poems, and have
adopted the voices of persons wholly different from me, including women.
Novelists do this sort of thing all the time, while many readers and critics
seem to deny this privilege to the poet, or to doubt that he is able to do it.
Some of the most grotesque misreadings of my poems have been made by
those who assume that all my poems are voiced *in propria persona.*

Of course, you haven't forsworn directly autobiographical material alto-

gether. In The Hard Hours, for example, there's 'Adam' and 'The Vow'. And at the very start of this interview I mentioned a poem I'll want to come back to in a moment, 'Apprehensions' ...

Certainly, you are right. One should feel free to choose a fictive or a personal voice according to one's needs, or even one's whims. It's also legitimate to leave the reader bewildered about just how personal any given poem may be. A good poet ought to be able to write both ways at will. Jim Wright could do so, and so, supremely well, could Robert Frost, whose 'Witch of Coös' is a wonderfully realized woman, utterly different from the poet. But that's not the end of the puzzle. After reading *Madame Bovary*, and meditating on Flaubert's declaration, 'Madame Bovary, c'est moi,' I construed that claim to mean that the novelist had so fully come to understand and empathize with his protagonist as to be able to render her thoughts and feelings with a rare fidelity. It was, I assumed, the writer's capacity to identify himself completely with another, no matter how different from himself. But in his splendid book, *Flaubert and Madame Bovary*, Francis Steegmuller suggests something far more curiously intimate, however well veiled. After his accounts of the young Madame Delamare, of Louise Colet, of Madame Pradier, Steegmuller goes on to say, 'But by now the largest part of Emma's character was being modelled on that of someone whom Flaubert knew far better than he knew any of those ladies. "*I* am Madame Bovary" – *Madame Bovary, c'est moi!* – the retort he would soon be making to anyone who asked him the identity of his model, could have been made now. "One no longer makes mistakes about the things of the soul": that was why *Madame Bovary* was coming true.' What I think this means is that there must be some part of any writer that goes into the creations of his characters, however alien from himself they may seem. And this must be true even of Shakespeare's most irredeemable villains – Iago, Edmund, King Claudius. What Steegmuller implies about Flaubert is not unconnected with the fact that he never married, and was uncommonly close to his mother, to whom he wrote, 'I kiss you till you suffocate: ... How darling your letters are! I devour them like a starving man. Adieu – a thousand more kisses!'

In 1971, still Professor of Rhetoric and Poetry at Rochester, you remarried, and won a Fulbright Scholarship which took you to Brazil. Did you visit Elizabeth Bishop while you were there?

No; she was not there. We saw her somewhere in the States, and she was kind enough to offer us the use of her place in Ouro Prêto, which we declined in part because it was rather out of the way, and I had a busy schedule of official duties in locations firmly fixed upon. I found out later that once she had made the same generous offer to Julian Beck and the members of the Living Theater, who got busted for drugs while living in her place, so her offer to us was brave as well as generous.

How well did you get to know Bishop? And how highly do you rate her poetic achievement?

I rate her very high. She is quite simply one of the finest American poets of this century. I don't remember how and where we first met, though I know we served on a number of literary juries together (one of them for the National Book Award, which went to James Merrill), and we saw something of each other during the term I taught in Harvard, where she also was teaching. We visited her out at Duxbury, Massachusetts, at the house of John Malcolm Brinnin, which he had lent to her.

The translation you and Helen Bacon did of Aeschylus's Seven Against Thebes *came out in 1973. What differences, if any, do you think working on that translation made to the character of your own writing?*

I am, in retrospect, not at all happy about that translation, but I think I learned a great deal about Aeschylus and about Greek tragedy.

What is it that displeases you?

The real language of Aeschylus is very strange: it's compact, jammed with metaphor, elliptical, anything but colloquial. It was mocked by Aristophanes for this very reason. The problem, which I failed to solve, was to find an idiom in English that could be intelligible to a modern theatre audience and still seem as freighted as the Greek. But such compressed and dense language would probably sound like unrelenting Hopkins or some of the more congested parts of David Jones's *In Parenthesis*. Nothing, in any case, that would be easily accessible to a theatre audience. My own English lines are rigid and stilted, and unconvincing. I did contribute my mite to the composition of the Introduction, and I am pleased with some light I hope to have shed upon this very puzzling and difficult play.

Did you ever try your hand again, at other pieces of classical theatre? Or had this one experience been enough?

Despite my disappointment in my own work on the play, I was

excited enough to want to tackle Sophocles's *Oedipus at Colonus*, which I worked on with William Arrowsmith. We got about half way through the first draft by the time he died, having often been drawn apart from one another and away from the task by other demands. Once again I felt I had learned enormously from my collaborator; and this time I felt a little better about my part in what we did. But, alas, it came to nothing, and now it never will.

Nine years separated the publication of The Hard Hours *and your third collection,* Millions of Strange Shadows. *This was the first of your books I ever read — led to it by the glowing review George P. Elliott did for the TLS — and it still occupies a special place in my affections.*
   Maybe I could ask you about 'Apprehensions', which contrasts in an interesting way with 'The Hill'. In the earlier poem, the speaker recalls walking through a sunlit and busy piazza only to have this disappear and be replaced by a sunless and desolate landscape, one he found deeply disturbing. In the later poem, the speaker recalls a troubled and unhappy childhood, only then to remember a moment of unalloyed happiness, when he'd stood at an open window and been transfixed by the changing light of a coming storm:

> *A storm was coming up by dark gradations.*
> *But what was curious about this was*
> *That as the sky seemed to be taking on*
> *An ashy blankness, behind which there lay*
> *Tonalities of lilac and dusty rose*
> *Tarnishing now to something more than dusk,*
> *Crepuscular and funerary greys,*
> *The streets became more luminous, the world*
> *Glinted and shone with an uncanny freshness.*
> *The brickwork of the house across the street*
> *(A grim, run-down Victorian chateau)*
> *Became distinct and legible; the air,*
> *Full of excited imminence, stood still.*
> *The streetcar tracks gleamed like the paths of snails.*
> *And all of this made me superbly happy,*
> *But most of all a yellow Checker Cab*
> *Parked at the corner. Something in the light*
> *Was making this the yellowest thing on earth.*
> *It was as if Adam, having completed*
> *Naming the animals, had started in*

On colours, and had found his primary pigment
Here, in a taxi cab, on Eighty-ninth street.
It was the absolute, parental yellow.

When talking about moments like these, some of your critics have reached for the word 'epiphany', but I wonder if you share my doubts about the word's appropriateness? It's normally used in connection with experiences which are revelatory — confronting us with the true nature of things — while, whatever their power to disturb or enchant, the experiences you recount don't seem to be revelatory in this sense. Or am I missing something?

No, I think you're right; there is no revelation, just an altered state of mind. Someone I know who had scientific information at hand, told me that in fact in the light that precedes a thunderstorm the colour yellow becomes more vivid, and that there's a scientific explanation for this. Your juxtaposition of 'Apprehensions' with 'A Hill' seems to me shrewd and right: their emotional trajectories turn in opposite directions. No one, as far as I know, has pointed this out before. And while I agree with you about the absence of epiphanies, I think there may be some connection with the idea of 'looking' as a crucially important act. At the end of 'The Venetian Vespers' the speaker (who is a composite person, partly my brother, much more a man I knew in Italy) says, 'I look and look, / As though I could be saved simply by looking ...' Simone Weil wrote that 'looking is what saves us,' and Ruskin declared, 'The greatest thing a human soul ever does in this world is to see something, and tell what it saw in a plain way. Hundreds of people can talk for one who can think, but thousands can think for one who can see. To see clearly is poetry, prophecy, and religion all in one' *(Modern Painters)*. One of the things I think I learned from Bishop, from Hardy, from Frost, concerned particularity and clarity of seeing. Seen with enough precision, things become wonderful, and one can see a world in a grain of sand. Bishop indeed alludes to Blake's line about the grain of sand in her poem 'Sandpiper,' and again and again in her poems she holds things up 'close to the eye.' I feel compelled to add that this was not a faculty with which I was endowed. It took conscious pains to acquire. In this I find myself in agreement with Matisse, who said, 'To see is itself a creative operation, requiring effort.'

The topic of looking came up in the interview you gave Langdon Hammer back in '96. On that occasion too you quoted Weil's remark about looking being what saves us, but you then went on to say something I thought very interesting: 'Surely part of that "salvation" is engendered by a capacity, at least momentarily, to forget ourselves, and fully to attend to something else.' In trying to explain this, you referred to something Auden once wrote, in an essay entitled 'Pride and Prayer':

> *'To pray is to pay attention to, or shall we say, to "listen" to someone or something other than oneself. Whenever a man so concentrates his attention – be it on a landscape or a poem or a geometrical problem or an idol or the True God – that he completely forgets his own ego and desires in listening to what the other has to say to him, he is praying.'*

Auden's thinking on this matter seems to be heavily indebted to Weil – the words could almost have been taken from Gravity and Grace – but rather than come full circle, you try to complete your explanation by referring to one of Pascal's pensées, which you judge to be equivalent in meaning to Auden's description of prayer: 'Le moi est haïssable.' Now, I'd like to ask why it is you think the self hateful, or, to put the same question slightly differently, why it is you think self-forgetfulness is so blessed a state. I assume that it's not because you think the self distracting, like a fly buzzing around one's study, making concentration difficult, but, rather, because you think the self corrupt, so constituted as to sully any looking that is not self-forgetful? That, at any rate, is one natural way of reading lines like these:

> *Here is the microscope one had as a child,*
> *The Christmas gift of some forgotten uncle.*
> *Here is the slide with a drop of cider vinegar*
> *As clear as gin, clear as your early mind.*
> *Look down, being most careful not to see*
> *Your own eye in the mirror underneath,*
> *Which will appear, unless your view is right,*
> *As a darkness on the face of the first waters.*

These lines are taken from one of the most distinguished, and haunting, of the poems in Millions of Strange Shadows, *'Green: An Epistle', which goes on to paint a truly disturbing picture of the self's development:*

> *Whole eras, seemingly without event,*
> *Now scud the glassy pool processionally*

Until one day, misty, uncalendared,
As mild and unemphatic as a schwa,
Vascular tissue, conduit filaments,
Learn how to feed the outposts of that small
Emerald principate. Now there are roots,
The filmy gills of toadstools, crested fern,
Quillworts, and foxtail mosses, and at last
Snapweed, loment, trillium, grass, herb Robert.
How soundlessly, shyly this came about,
One thinks today. But that is not the truth.
It was, from the first, an everlasting war
Conducted, as always, at gigantic cost.
Think of the droughts, the shifts of wind and weather,
The many seeds washed to some salt conclusion
Or brought to rest at last on barren ground.
Think of some inching tendrils worming down
In hope of water, blind and white as death.
Think of the strange mutations life requires.
Only the toughest endured, themselves much altered,
Trained in the cripple's careful sciences
Of mute accommodation. The survivors
Were all, one way or another, amputees
Who learned to live with their stumps, like
      Breughel's beggars.

This will require a complicated answer. Your point of departure is something I said in an interview with Langdon Hammer, who was asking me about 'looking', with particular regard to two poems of mine, 'The Venetian Vespers' and 'Meditation'. He even quoted a line or so from 'Vespers', to which I responded with those comments from Weil, Auden and Pascal. Your question, however, seems to appropriate my response to Hammer and to apply it to another poem, 'Green: An Epistle'. If this procedure is not entirely wrong, neither is it entirely right. Let me try to explain. 'The Venetian Vespers' is about an invented character, largely a man I knew in Ischia, partly my brother, and necessarily something of myself. But for the most part, the character is invented. He is a deeply troubled, neurotic, hampered man, and his misery only exacerbates his self-concern. This is a common enough form of mental behaviour. In one of his stories called 'Enemies', Chekhov writes, 'In both men the egotism of the unhappy was powerfully evident. Unhappy people are egotistical, mean, unjust, cruel and less capable than stupid people of understanding each other. Rather than bringing people together, unhappiness drives them further apart, and even where it would seem that people ought to be joined by a similar cause of sorrow, they make themselves much more injustice and cruelty than in an environment in which people are relatively contented.' My speaker in 'Vespers' is alert enough about himself to recognize the egotism engendered by his unhappiness, and to want to escape from it by 'looking', as Weil and Auden hinted that he might.

But you go on to pose this question: 'I'd like to ask why it is you think the self is hateful, or, to put the same question slightly differently, why it is that you think self-forgetfulness is so blessed a state.' And in proposing this question, you have in mind some lines from 'Green', and not just some lines, but indeed the main thrust of the poem. I can make a start by saying that I myself as an acknowledged voice and presence am far more involved in 'Green' than I am aware of being in 'Vespers'. And 'Green' is, like 'Vespers', about the infections of the ego. To write carefully about this problem may be beyond the proper limits of an interview such as this, but I'll make a stab at it.

That rather pathetic poseuse, Edith Sitwell, once declared, 'Pride has always been one of my favourite virtues. I have never regarded it, except in certain cases, as a major sin.' But I find myself more in accord with the Church Fathers, with Milton, and others who find Pride the most radical, pervasive, and nearly ineradicable of all the sins. And this is so because Pride is capable of so many ingenious and unlikely disguises. That cool, unsentimental moralist, La Rochefoucauld, observed, 'Self-interest speaks all sorts of languages and plays all sorts of roles, even that of disinterestedness.' Our capacity to think well of ourselves is versatile to the point of monstrosity. And this is probably true even of those widely regarded as wicked. They would number among themselves the 'progressive tyrants', those who put into effect the Soviet Five-Year Plans and the Chinese 'Great Leap Forward', social programs of great human cost, undertaken in behalf of some impossible utopian ideal. And of course there are others among the wicked who feel no personal responsibility for their crimes, blaming society or their parents for any of their misdeeds.

Pride can disguise itself as humility, or more accurately, some kind of false humility. And it is not always so transparent as in the case of Uriah Heep. I know quite a number of people who quietly pride themselves on what they find in themselves as a modest and unassuming character; they are deeply tainted with a moral smugness they cannot for the life of them recognize. It may be that as in those infinitely regressive images of oneself that can be seen in the facing mirrors of a haberdasher, the nearest image of oneself might be regarded as the most patent kind of false-humility. But as the images recede, getting smaller and further away, it becomes more difficult to tell where falsity leaves off and the genuine begins. Even self-hatred can serve as one of egotism's disguises, and it does so, I believe, in *Crime and Punishment*. Raskolnikov is thought, even by himself, to have committed his crime out of a sense of superiority, of being a superman: in a word, of pride. It's possible he believes this, and there's no doubt many literary critics and commentators on the novel believe it; and the novel furnishes many examples of Raskolnikov's egotism and pride. But near the end (Chapter VII, Part Six) this hero thinks to himself (in the Coulson translation, with the emphasis in the text itself), 'I am cruel, I know. But why should they love me so much, when I am not worthy of it? Oh, if only I were alone and nobody loved me, and I had never loved anyone! *All this would never have happened.*'

Now, 'Green: An Epistle' is about the disguises of Pride. It is about how attempts to suppress the ego in behalf of some idealism or the desire to appear kind and generous will quietly and all unbeknownst to someone convert that suppression into a corruption of the soul, a deformity of spirit, and the longer the suppression goes on the more martyred and selfless one feels, and the more monstrous the deformity. The universal desire to think well of ourselves almost invariably involves the suppression of memory as well. Almost everyone commits foolish or unkind acts of which they are ashamed; and the normal reaction is to forget them. Freud has a lot to say about memory lapses, but it may be added that there is something profoundly merciful about the myth of the River Lethe, with its healing relief from the painful memories of our follies as well as our more serious failures.

Self-forgetfulness can be achieved in many ways, and there are those so agonized with physical, mental or spiritual pain that they seek some kind of oblivion. Drugs and drink are commonly employed; anaesthesia is often welcomed. The longed-for death in certain of Eliot's poems, the comfort of death in *The Waste Land*, where it is said that 'Winter kept us warm, covering / Earth in forgetful snow,' makes clear how desirable is forgetfulness.

The speaker in my poem, 'Green', who is admittedly partly me, has succeeded in deceiving himself into believing that his long-suffering patience and forbearance, his stoic endurance, have paid off in the form of a noble and selfless character, and in this he is profoundly mistaken.

In your conversation with Langdon Hammer, you expressed a worry about Auden's definition of prayer, the worry, namely, that it takes no account of the self-forgetful person's cause, where he or she has such a thing. The unmixed attention of a surgeon can perhaps be called prayer, but what about the unmixed attention of the torturer? And there's a related worry, or set of worries, which I can best get at by quoting from another very accomplished poem in The Hard Hours, 'Ostia Antica'. The poem centres on an incident described by St. Augustine in Book IX of The Confessions. The scene is 4th century Ostia Antica, not far from Rome. Augustine and his mother are waiting for a boat that will return them to Africa, and have been engaged in a conversation about time and eternity, a conversation which gradually takes on the most extraordinary character:

'And when our conversation had arrived at that point, that the very highest pleasure of the carnal senses, and that in the very brightest material light, seemed by reason of the sweetness of that life not only not worthy of comparison, but not even of mention, we, lifting ourselves with a more ardent affection towards "the self-same", did gradually pass through all corporeal things, and even the heaven itself, whence sun, and moon, and stars shine upon the earth; yea, we soared higher yet by inward musing, and discoursing, and admiring Thy works; and we came to our own minds, and went beyond them, that we might advance as high as that region of unfailing plenty, where Thou feedest Israel for ever with the food of truth, and where life is that Wisdom by whom all these things are made, both which have been, and which are to come; and she is not made, but is as she hath been, and so shall ever be; yea, rather, to "have been", and "to be hereafter", are not in her, but only "to be", seeing she is eternal, for to "have been" and "to be hereafter" are not eternal. And while we were thus speaking, and straining after her, we slightly touched her with the whole effort of our heart; and we sighed, and there left bound "the first fruits of the Spirit"; and returned to the noise of our own mouth, where the word uttered has both beginning and end.'

The first six stanzas of 'Ostia Antica' give us a panoramic view of Ostia – though that's a poor way to describe lines as rich and suggestive as these – and then, in the sixth and seventh stanzas, the focus narrows, and what we read are the words of Augustine and his mother, now self-aware again, but meditating on the significance of that extraordinary moment of self-forgetfulness:

'If there were hushed
To us the images of earth, its poles
Hushed, and the waters of it,
And hushed the tumult of the flesh, even
The voice intrinsic of our souls,
Each tongue and token hushed and the long habit
Of thought, if that first light, the given
To us were hushed,

So that the washed
Object, fixed in the sun, were dumb,
And to the mind its brilliance
Were from beyond itself, and the mind were clear
As the unclouded dome
Wherein all things diminish, in that silence
Might we not confidently hear
God as he wished?'

The poem could almost have ended there, but it doesn't. There's one more stanza, and that stanza dramatically unsettles our perspective on all that's gone before:

Then from the grove
Suddenly falls a flight of bells.
A figure moves from the wood,
Darkly approaching at the hour of vespers
Along the ruined walls.
And bearing heavy articles of blood
And symbols of endurance, whispers,
'This is love.'

Of course, it's possible to interpret these lines in very different ways, but no matter which way we read them, it seems to me that they make plain the importance of the larger view, a view which takes in not just causes but also consequences ...

First of all, let me say that in quoting Augustine's Confessions, the passage you select is from Book IX, chapter x, paragraph 24. But the two stanzas of my poem that you quote are a verse paraphrase of the paragraph following that, paragraph 25. The translation I believe I used for the poem was that of J.G. Pilkington.

The poem was written at one of the most troubled and unhappy periods of my life. Normally, when I am deeply depressed I can't write at all, so the existence of this poem is, in a purely private way, a kind of miracle. It undertakes to bring into some conjunction three kinds of love. The first is a heedless, more or less innocent hedonistic and erotic love, one that takes eager pleasure in all the luxurious capacities of the senses, not omitting the sheer delight in 'seeing'. The second is the transcendent, immaterial love of which Santa Monica and her son speak, and which I try to paraphrase. The third is the self-immolating and sacrificial love of Christ. Just in what way these three modes of love applied to me in my tormented quandary I cannot now say with assurance. But at the time I felt as though their contradictory, or at least diverse, impulses were not only at work within me, but dividing me against myself.

There is one part of your question that invites some sort of elaboration from me in response. You ask, 'The unmixed attention of a surgeon can perhaps be called prayer, but what about the unmixed attention of the torturer?' The torturer is a special and especially ghoulish case, because he is right there, and can't avoid knowing what he's doing. But special though the case may be, the Third Reich seemed to have no difficulty in finding plenty of staff to run the camps. But the problem is made more difficult when we come to those bureaucrats like Eichmann, and many other paper-shufflers below him and beside him, who took a statistical view of their labours and duties. They are not completely to be distinguished from the bombardiers who do not see the result of their handiwork.

As for your comment that the final stanza of the poem brings it to a new and unexpected element, I think you are right. It introduces *pain* where there had been none before. It is pain that might be redemptive, but just possibly might not. This was a quandary, and a torment in which, for a long time, I dwelt.

There's a fine poem in Millions of Strange Shadows *which seems not to have attracted much attention. I'm thinking of 'Swan Dive', which is as good a description of a dive — both from a diver's point of view, and an onlooker's — as I'm able to imagine. It's another of the poems in which you explore discontinuities of one kind or another, and I wonder if you can explain the attraction these discontinuities have for you?*

First of all, I'm gratified that you like the poem, not only because I rather like it myself, but because it was singled out for abuse by a reviewer, who said something like: in this poem we are told more about diving than we want to know. Discontinuities; yes. I believe they are a factor in my poems right from the first. Certainly in 'A Hill', and probably everywhere. This is, perhaps I can say, quasi-deliberate. What I mean is that when I first started to write poems there was an orthodoxy about what the 'lyric' was (and the 'lyric' was regarded as pretty much anything that wasn't 'epic'.) I've looked up some definitions in poetry handbooks, and they all seem to agree that it is a short poem 'in which a single perception or feeling is overtly expressed.' The lyric was understood to be a pure instant of perception captured in the course of its fleeting evanescence; it was a rapid sketch of some state of the soul, a hasty impression of the receptive mind, more inward than outward, often taking some grain of reality as a point of departure into a state of private rapture. A good deal of lousy poetry was written on this principle, and still is. But I resisted the principle from the first, not initially on any theoretical basis, but because some of the poetry I first fell in love with was the work of John Donne, whose poems are filled with jostling paradox and ironic self-contradiction, and which were, moreover, highly dramatic, and such drama, however minimal, required something like oppositions and complexities that the 'lyric', as I had heard it defined, very specifically lacked. My instincts told me that, for me, Donne's kind of poetry was more attractive, more exciting and interesting than some simple *cri du coeur*. But I guess I ought also to confess that I did not trust my own feelings enough to risk such a *cri du coeur*, and I sought protection in dramatic structures and irony. On the whole, I think I chose the right path for me, and I still find lyrics written according to the old ideal boring, when not self-consciously posturing and narcissistic. In his biography of Oscar Wilde, Richard Ellmann writes: 'We live in age when men treat art as if it were meant to be a form of autobiography ... Poets know how useful passion is for publication. Nowadays a broken heart will run into many editions.'

Even very friendly critics have sometimes baulked at your vocabulary. I'm reminded of this now by your use in 'Swan Dive' of the word 'anthelions', which, though not Latinate *or* précieux *— two of the terms I have seen used in this connection — is likely to have most people reaching for their dictionaries the first time they come across it. Now, I think I'm right in saying that there is no other word in English which does the job you want this one to do. All the same, I wonder if you ever worry about using words like this, words whose unfamiliarity makes them stand out?*

Well, when you first are introduced to poetry and find that the most admired poets use words like 'polyphiloprogenitive' and 'piaculative' or 'dedolant', 'mornes and motted mammelons', and 'jussive', or even Ransom's 'pernoctated,' or Thomas Hardy's 'heart-hydromels', you tend to a certain boldness in these matters. Doubtless there's a little defiance in it; a tiny flavour of Joyce's taunt that it took him twenty years to write *Finnegans Wake*, and he expected readers to take just as long to read it. The defiance is also probably a reaction to the public's comparative indifference to poetry in general — a forlorn resignation to a minority readership, the more élite the better, since there's not much choice in the matter. There's nothing wrong with inviting a reader to look up a word. He has to do so when reading a lot of early poetry where obsolete language often can't be understood without a little research.

Your next collection, The Venetian Vespers, *appeared just two years after* Millions of Strange Shadows, *in 1979, but I assume it had been in preparation for a lot longer than that?*

No, it was composed with a blessed speed, rarely available to me.

It was the first of your volumes to have notes appended to it. What prompted the departure, I wonder?

The notes, like the epigraphs, are later embellishments, after the poem has been completed. I think I can explain their appearances at a certain point by the fact that just around the time I decided to introduce them, or to indicate the sources of the epigraphs, I was doing a lot of public poetry reading. Reading a poem aloud to an audience is a totally different business from allowing them to read it at their leisure in the comfort of their homes. They have no time to mull over individual lines, look up unfamiliar words, track down the sources of quotations. And I found increasingly that before reading a poem aloud I would try to supply the kind of information that would allow a listener to remain comparatively untroubled by whatever obstacles the poem presented. And from there it was but a step to including this information in the form of notes.

You mentioned your epigraphs, and I'd like to ask why it is that their provenance is sometimes explained, and sometimes not. In 'The Venetian Vespers', for example, we are told that the quotations come from Othello *and* The Stones of Venice, *while in 'The Short End', we are not told that the quotation comes from 'The Phoenix and the Turtle'. Is there a rationale behind this? If so, can you tell me what it is, because the obvious explanation — that some of your sources are less likely to be recognized than others — doesn't seem to work.*

When an epigraph appears without any source, it is because I hope the reader will recognize its (usually Biblical) origin. I was bold enough to think that 'The Phoenix and the Turtle' would be known to many readers, but even if it wasn't, the incinerating imagery of the stanza quoted would be intelligible to a reader of my own poem. As for 'Vespers', I wanted the Ruskin sentence because its calm tone of pastoral resignation would contrast with the tone of my own, very urban poem, and I did not think it so well known as to expect a reader at once to identify it. And if I was to identify the Ruskin, I could not leave the *Othello* lines unidentified, if only for consistency's sake, though the lines are by no means the best known in the play.

J.D. McClatchy described 'The Short End' as a 'nasty, brutal, long poem,' doubtless intending to remind his readers of Hobbes's famous description of mortal life. And the reminder is entirely appropriate, because Shirley Carson's life can indeed be thought 'solitary, poor, nasty, brutish, and short,' even if we might want to resist the idea of its being in any way typical or representative. What is it about a figure like Shirley that attracts the writer in you? With her love of schlock, her dependence on alcohol and cigarettes, and so on, she isn't an easy person to identify with, is she?

First of all, there's a large literature about 'grotesques'. Dostoievski is full of them. So is Dickens, whom Dostoievski admired. So is Faulkner and Flannery O'Connor. No-one ever thinks it odd that a novelist, whose purview embraces as wide a variety of humanity as possible, should interest himself in the marginal lives of the less favoured. In one of his poems Auden has some lines about looking at the faces of strangers in the subway, and trying to figure out what forces went into determining their fates, and the very faces themselves. Surely this is a natural sort of inquiry. All the time we see around us figures of desperation and despair, and wonder not only what brought them to this pass, but what life for them might have been like earlier, when they were full of hopes and expectations.

I didn't mean to suggest that Shirley was an inappropriate subject for you to tackle, or even an especially odd one. I just wondered what it was about her that appealed to you.

74

I chose Shirley precisely because she was so unprepossessing, so unlikely to enlist the sympathy of the reader; and I set it as a challenge to myself to try, before the poem closed, to earn some measure of compassion for her. Moreover, I think this is not an uncommon goal for certain writers. I've already mentioned some novelists (to which list more could be added) but there are poets who have been lured by the same challenge. Consider James Wright's touching 'Two Poems About President Harding', which undertakes to elicit compassion for a rogue political figure. Still more ambitious in this regard is Wright's 'At the Executed Murderer's Grave'. (Incidentally, Wright did his doctoral dissertation on Dickens.) Think of Snodgrass's entire sequence, *The Führer Bunker*. Who could find a more forbidding, less alluring cast of characters? Think of a whole host of Browning's protagonists, not excluding Mr Sludge and the Duke of Ferrara. Of course, I have seen such women as Shirley appears to be when we first meet her in the poem, and I have furnished her (I use the word with care) with appropriate adornments, like the pillows (though how she came by anything so classy as a Biedermeier I'm not sure I can explain). But many of these items are omens which are important to the poem, and to poor Shirley's fate. The New York World's Fair, for example, did in reality have the motto of 'A Century of Progress', in spite of the fact that it took place in 1939, the year WWII began, though the signs of its approach had been visible for some time. (If I may interject a curious fact about the fair, someone noticed, after it had been running for a while, that the red star held aloft by a stainless steel worker at the top of the Soviet building was the highest thing in the fair. Much consternation. What to do? The problem was at length patriotically resolved by putting an American flag on the top of the parachute jump in the mid-way entertainment section of the fair, where the roller-coaster and Ferris wheels were located, and which was a few inches taller than the Soviet star.) Also, in the mid-thirties, under Roosevelt, much legislation was passed to cope with unemployment, to guarantee fair wages and social security, and many were living in perilous financial uncertainty. It may be that my own father's career, or the anxiety it produced in me, figures in some obscure way in this poem. (To this day, to the surprise and mild amusement of my wife and son, I routinely wander the house turning off lights in rooms where they have been left on by someone who has left, and performing other small acts of compulsive frugality.) Anyway, there were men in those years who tried to earn a livelihood by sitting for record lengths at the tops of flag-poles; they were actually called *flag-pole sitters*, as though it were a recognized profession. They were secular Simeon Styliteses. There were also those who buried themselves alive, like the

George Rose in my poem. (His name, incidentally, comes from Baron Corvo's *Hadrian the Seventh*, though I intend no papal or even literary allusion. He is George Rose for my purposes because in due course he will rise again when they dig him up and count their earnings.) Poverty, anyway, or at least a shabby mode of life, was something I was aiming at. And this was because I explicitly intended this longish poem to balance another in the same book, 'The Venetian Vespers.' The second of these (which was written first) had a male protagonist, so 'The Short End' was given over to a female. The Venetian poem had a certain sumptuousness to it, so the companion poem was to be stark and barren by comparison. The two poems are also opposed in that one is set in America and the other abroad. All this was conscious and deliberate. There is one more thing worth mention. The poem was written just after I had quit smoking, after having been a heavy smoker for thirty-five years; the poem is thus a kind of exorcism of a defeated vice. As a recovered smoker, I was a particularly vigorous and zealous convert to the camp of pulmonary and cardiac virtue, a sort of St. Paul-of-the-Lungs. Hence the terrible death to which I consigned Shirley.

The Vietnam War had made its presence felt in your previous collection, in 'The Odds', but it's there as backdrop, not as subject. In the later collection, it does appear as subject, in 'An Overview', which contrasts the north Vietnam of the bomber crews', the general staff's and the President's imaginings — distance of one kind or another having lent it the enchantment of a toy kingdom — with the bloodied reality. Might I ask how the war impinged on you, as private individual and as public figure?

It was a strange, troubled and wrenching period in America. Thinking back on it now, I can remember only one person who fully supported the war in Vietnam, and I discovered this under circumstances that exposed us both to some embarrassment. He was older than I, and a conservative businessman. We were both members of a club, and I spoke critically of the war, supposing no one would disagree. But he was deeply affronted, and said so loudly and at length. For a while I thought he was a mindless zealot, but it turned out that his only son had been killed in the war, and to admit to himself that the whole bungled and hopeless campaign was doomed was more than he could bear. He had to believe in eventual victory, if only to justify his son's death. This kind of mental attitude is all too common in war-time, and the army is invariably eager for early military heroes, especially dead ones. Nothing can make the home front more implacable than unwillingness to admit that its most terrible sacrifices have been in vain. But that is only part of the story. Opposed as I was to every aspect of the war, I was also determined not to rant and rave in public poetry readings on the subject, which was ultimately only a kind of self-promotion. There were not a few poets in those years who literally got their pictures in the papers for resisting arrest at anti-war demonstrations. Such arrests did nothing to impede the war effort, nor introduce a moment's doubt in the minds of Henry Kissinger or the president. A number of my fellow teachers found a curious academic mode of war-resistance. They quietly but resolutely gave no poor grades to any male students that might jeopardize their draft status by academic failure. It was probably, in the light of all the deaths and casualties of that war, a feeble gesture, though it almost certainly saved more lives than all the anti-war poetry readings combined.

How upset are you when you find your poems misread? I'm minded to ask you this now because of something Robert von Hallberg said about the poem I mentioned just now, 'An Overview'. Having quoted from one of Bly's war poems, and one of Duncan's — the former calling Dean Rusk a bomb waiting to be loaded, the latter claiming to find the glint of Satan's eyes first in Barry Goldwater's, and then in Lyndon Johnson's — he goes on to say: 'Later came moments of greater leniency, as when Anthony Hecht in 1978 wrote of the "engaging roguishness" of the young bomber pilots who flew so high above their targets that they could not appreciate the suffering they were causing.' Von Hallberg seems to think that, because you don't deny their humanity, you are being less hard on the pilots than Bly and Duncan were on the politicians. So far as I can see, this is the very reverse of the truth ...

You are perfectly right; and von Hallberg is wrong. To begin with your initial question about how upset I get when my poems are misread, I can say that I've grown more inured to it, though it's always painful. One critic asseverated (it's the only word I can use) that 'Green: An Epistle' was 'about the colour green' ...

As Sydney Smith might have said, 'I never read a poem before writing about it; it prejudices a man so.'

As for those young pilots in my poem 'An Overview,' one of the points I was trying to make, not clearly enough for Mr von Hallberg, who doesn't seem to recognize irony, was that technological warfare has developed in such a way as to permit killing at distances that keep the enemy out of actual sight, and thus minimize the anguish and guilt a warrior would otherwise feel. I go into this at some length in my book on Auden, and in regard to his poem 'The Shield of Achilles', which contrasts the heroic confrontations of *The Iliad* with the impersonal, technological warfare of modern times in which, by means of 'smart bombs' and other cunning devices, we are kept from feeling the impact of what we are doing. 'Engaging roguishness' is only possible for bombardiers or their pilots when they are protected from seeing the results of their actions. Army lingo, even Defence Department statements, are full of euphemisms, meant to conceal the full emotional and literal truth of what is being said. There are now 'soft' and 'hard' targets, the latter being military installations, vehicles, cities, infrastructures, and the former being human bodies. All war bulletins are couched in these evasions. But, again, better poets than I have been misread, so I suppose I can't complain. I'm not acquainted with the poems by Bly and Duncan that von Hallberg so much admires, but I must say that I have little sympathy or patience with the poetry of moral indignation. What's wrong with it is that it conveniently and neatly divides the moral universe into good and bad, right and wrong, and is predicated on the perfect righteousness of the indignant speaker.

I recently came across an uncollected poem of yours which dates from 1972 and shows just how unsympathetic and impatient you were with the protest poetry of the day:

> Here lies fierce Strephon, whose poetic rage
> Lashed out on Vietnam from page and stage;
> Whereby from basements of Bohemia he
> Rose to the lofts of sweet celebrity,
> Being, by Fortune, (our Eternal Whore)
> One of the few to profit by that war,
> A fate he shared – it bears much thinking on –
> With certain persons at the Pentagon.

Thank you for exhuming those buried lines. They do indeed express my impatience of those years with indignant, sanctimonious poets. Even when a poem's speaker is, by common consent, in the right, this is uninteresting because he is preaching to the converted, and because his poem lacks the drama of antithesis, or the antinomies that Yeats so rightly and shrewdly cherished. Yeats, too, along with Donne, was a formative force in my understanding of how poems work. The majesty of a poem like Yeats's

'Easter 1916' is due to his full awareness that both action and inaction in public affairs, and in military ones in particular, are compromised positions, and that there are no clear, unambiguous solutions to the moral dilemmas of life. Anyway, my air force boys are happy-go-lucky (a) because their height in the sky protects them from seeing the effects of what they're doing, and (b) because all soldiers in modern warfare require some psychic refuge from the ferocity of their own actions. This is essential to keep from going crazy. I ought to know.

Can you tell me about the genesis of 'The Venetian Vespers' — what sparked it off, how long it was in the making, how the six-part structure was arrived at?

A big topic. And not easy accurately to reconstruct at this distance in time. There was — there *is* the city itself, the decayed magnificence, now the centre of tourist pilgrimage as once it was the centre of religious pilgrimage and of commerce, the latter two intimately combined (as they are in *The Merchant of Venice*). I wanted to write a poem that would capture some of this brilliance and decay, and in thinking it over I recalled the story of the man whom I adopted as the poem's speaker. He was someone I had met in Ischia, a deeply tormented, morally agonized man whose family story is substantially the one told in my poem. The actual man, my model, was a rigid vegetarian, who would not eat eggs unless they could be demonstrated to be infertile. He suffered from terrible boils, like Job, and was, when I first knew him, a touching, gentle man. Later in his life he became a photographer for *Life* magazine, and, though still a vegetarian, rather less vulnerable and sympathetic. But at the time I wrote the poem I did not know this. There is also a component of my brother's suffering in the character I created. It seemed to me that this man, nameless in my poem, in his illness and stoic resolve was a kind of figuration of the city in its decay, its lingering on from greatness to a tourist attraction, yet with an undeniable dignity and beauty for all that. My intention was to braid these twin elements, man and city, so that the reader would feel them to be appropriately matched. It was written quite rapidly. I was surprised myself. I think it was done in a couple of months. I guess I should add, what may be obvious, that a few details in the poem come out of my own experience, in combat in the army and in Gracey Square Hospital. As for the division of the poem into six parts, and what went into each one, I'm afraid I can only say that the poem is meant to develop incrementally, slowly and with a degree of mystery about it. Whether or not I've succeeded must be left to others to judge.

J.D. McClatchy has an excellent essay on your work, entitled 'Anatomies of Melancholy'. But excellent though it is, the essay contains a line of argument which I find hard to accept, relating to some of the more richly descriptive passages in your writing. He's thinking of passages like the one in 'The Hill' where the speaker is describing the Piazza Farnese, and the one in 'The Venetian Vespers' where the speaker is describing the evening sky. Reflection on these and other passages — which he calls baroque or empurpled — has persuaded him that '[t]he extravagance of the high style in a Hecht poem should signal some unknowing desperation, some pride before a fall.' You resort to it, he says, 'usually as a deliberate thematic manoeuvre'. Now, I don't see any reason to believe this. I think you're only practising what you preached in 'On the Methods and Ambitions of Poetry', where you talked about a poem's paying homage to the natural world by striving to imitate it, even in its superfluity or excess of texture. McClatchy knows that essay, of course, and even cites this part of it, without any kind of demur. But it's as though he needs a better explanation for what you do at points like these, an explanation, perhaps, which will enable him to accept your high style without much liking it. What do you make of McClatchy's argument?

Will it seem like shameless equivocating if I say that you both seem to be right? There is a clear contrast in the diction of my poems between elaborate and simple speech, between the ornate, the compressed, the densely worked passage and the fluent, colloquial, and straightforward mode of parlance. This is conscious and deliberate. With regard specifically to 'A Hill', it was my intention to write about the Roman setting in manifestly metaphoric style, or, more accurately, in a language adorned with metaphor. The purpose is ironic. The use of such language is often reserved for descriptions of visionary experience and states of transport, while here they are used to describe a real and everyday experience, though, to be sure, a joyful one, but also one that is shortly to be contrasted with a genuine visionary experience, described in the almost unadorned language usually reserved for raw experience, untransformed by vision or by art. The juxtaposition of these two scenes is an instance of the kind of dialectic that is a normal part of the pattern of my poetry, and represents my rejection of the sort of 'lyric' that aims at a single effect or a single emotion. Extravagance is a legitimate feature of poetry — and not just in the effusions of Swinburne or the swoonings of Edna St. Vincent Millay. Stevens wrote somewhere about the 'essential gaudiness' of poetry, and the fastidious Marianne Moore admired its 'gusto'. For me, the extravagance, the embellishments, are often desirable in and for themselves; though I know perfectly well that there are superb poems by Frost composed in a Shaker plainness or Savonarolan austerity, unyielding to adornment throughout. These are simply different strategies. As for McClatchy's suspicion that the high style in my poems 'should signal some unknowing desperation,' he is certainly right to the extent that my instinct for contrast and dialectic is almost always at work, as a dramatic element of the poem, so that any flamboyance is likely to be confronted or opposed by counter-force, directness, elemental grit.

Which of today's critics do you read with the greatest enjoyment, and what is it that you get from them?

It is always hazardous to compose lists like this, and if you had asked me to name poets instead of critics I would probably have refused. But I can say with a sort of confidence that I continue to read Empson with delight, even when he is being crotchety and wrong-headed. He is always brilliant. To stick with the English, I would add Christopher Ricks and Frank Kermode and Tony Tanner. These writers seem to me fully alert at all times, widely read, careful in their judgements, solid in their scholarship. In America I would include Harold Bloom, John Hollander (who of course is also a poet) and Eleanor Cook.

Harold Bloom and John Hollander are both well-known in England, but the same isn't true of Eleanor Cook. Why, I'm not sure, because a book like Against Coercion *is clearly the work of a first-rate critic.*

All these writers, different from one another though they are, enliven the mind in astonishing and unexpected ways. They offer sustained acts of scrutiny and of careful focus, enriched and contextualized by great learning and a decent humanity. To read them is often to see what I had not myself had the patience, or wit, or scholarship to see; and to read them a second or third time is to marvel at the clarity and elegance of their perceptions.

You said just now that if I'd been asking you to name the poets, rather than the critics, you read with greatest enjoyment, you would probably have refused to do so. Why is this?

Because in the making of such lists there is almost always the danger of forgetting some important name, or even names, thereby leading old friends to think one no longer regards their work with approval. This has happened to me in the past, and I've become chary about repeating any such clumsiness. No matter how long the list was, I would be sure to omit a name or two. (I can add that my willingness to list my favourite critics is based on the supposition that they are more thick-skinned than poets, and don't in the least care, or seem to care, what poets think of them.)

According to Joel Brouwer, 'Poets have a responsibility to write serious reviews and essays about their contemporaries, even when the prospect seems daunting. Call it literary jury service.' Have you had to do much literary jury service over the years? I ask because the only reviews of yours I've seen are those in Obbligati.

Obbligati includes two book reviews that appeared in the *TLS*, one of Richard Wilbur and the other of Elizabeth Bishop. It also contains a lecture on Robert Lowell. For many years in the sixties I was poetry editor of *The Hudson Review*, and my duties included regular reviews of current poetry by such poets as: Pasternak, William Carlos Williams, a new translation of Adam Mickiewicz, Conrad Aiken, Edwin Muir, John Ciardi, Katherine Hoskins, Josephine Miles, Reed Whittemore, Tennessee Williams, Louis MacNeice, John Heath-Stubbs, David Wagoner, Donald Hall, a slim book of original poems by Vladimir Nabokov, Marianne Moore, Delmore Schwartz, Louis Simpson, James Wright, Jack Kerouac, Wallace Stevens, Robert Penn Warren, Richmond Lattimore, Howard Nemerov, James Merrill, Donald Finkel, John Haines, Jon Silkin, John Wain and Günter Grass. That is a partial list. More recently I have done book reviews for two Washington papers, as well as articles for *The Wilson Quarterly*, and these have dealt with: Ransom, Wilbur, Bishop, Moore, Brad Leithauser, Mark Strand, Jarrell, Tate, Eliot, Auden, Lowell, Montale, L.E. Sissman, Carl Dennis, Joseph Brodsky, George Starbuck, May Swenson, and Richard Howard. Less publicly, I have served on a considerable number of real literary juries that conferred such awards as the Pulitzer, the Bollingen, the National Book Award, as well as the awards annually bestowed by the American Academy of Arts and Letters.

There's an essay of Frank Kermode's, published in 1980, which begins as follows: 'It is a commonplace that over the past fifteen years or so we have witnessed extraordinary transformations in literary theory and critical method. Those who hoped to keep quiet, sit it out, and wait for a return to normal must now suppose that they have lost their wager. We have, without question, had some sort of revolution.' Can I ask about your outlook on this revolution?

The passage of Kermode that you quote is delicately non-committal. Though I've never known him to lose his gentlemanly poise, I have read views of his that indicate much more clearly where his sympathies lie. As for my own views, I think I've already indicated something of what I feel as it has affected English Departments (at least in America) and the ill effects of interdisciplinary promiscuity. Nothing I could add would much surprise you, but perhaps you will allow me to quote the admirable Harold Bloom, whose views of the matter agree conveniently with mine. He writes: 'Culturally, we are at Thermopylae: the multi-culturalists, the hordes of camp-followers afflicted with the French diseases, the mock feminists, the commissars, the gender-and-power freaks, the hosts of new historicists and old materialists — all stand below us. They will surge up and we may be overcome; our universities are already travesties, and our journalists parody our professors of "cultural studies" ... I have seen my profession dying for over a quarter century now, and in another decade it may be dead.' I'm not sure I can add anything to Bloom's catalogue of woes (though I can't fail to be struck by his anti-historical recasting of French diseases back to the time of Thermopylae). The crippling effects upon students of this disintegration has yet completely to be felt, though some of these students are now themselves faculty members, and thus the 'French diseases' spread. I can, however, give you a small instance of how these effects are now at work. A critic working on a volume of commentary on Baudelaire wrote to me to ask permission to quote a translation I had done of one of Baudelaire's sonnets. I granted permission without hesitation, though I knew nothing about the critic. In due course — which was a very long time, during which I had completely forgotten about the projected book — a complimentary copy reached me. It was a big, hefty book, and was published by a university press — though this last means nothing much as far as quality or interest is concerned. Anyway, the book was big, and I braced myself for the serious task of reading it. As with most such daunting books, I began with the index, the bibliography, the notes, then the chapter titles, and a brisk flip through the many pages. Whereupon, lo and behold, I discovered that my fourteen-line translation was the only poetry whatever, either in French or English, in the entire length of the book. A study of poetry that stays that far away from the texts it is putatively considering has no real concern for poems, and, as it quickly proved, this one was devoted virtually entirely to idle philosophic speculations and the mind-travels of the critic, who hastily left Baudelaire behind. The interdisciplinary promiscuity I deplore, and the muddles and outright fallacies it engenders are nothing new, merely more pervasive. Geoffrey Scott, in *The Architecture of Humanism* (1914), rejected the non-aesthetic criteria – derived from poetry, science, morals or philosophy – that debased architectural discourse, and led theorists into fanciful and profitless speculation. And in her fine book, *A Reading of George Herbert* (1952), Rosemund Tuve gently regretted the too rigorous or Procrustean application of Freudian dogmas to Herbert's poetry by Empson. She writes, ' ...if it is the theory we are chiefly excited about, the great thing will be to detect happily the traces of the theory in the work; it will not be the poem, and the poem's own *raison d'être*, which suddenly seem unreplaceably beautiful, and unendurably true – for it is not these which have had our attention. There is thus loss, though there is no great harm, in looking at plays and poems to see whether they know what we know. The harm comes when we become willing to overlook a certain amount of violence done to the play, done to the conception clearly central to the poet, done to the theme, to the image – in the interest of finding in a piece the clichés of our own favoured patterns.'

One could be forgiven for thinking that the passage you quoted a moment ago was from Allan *rather than* Harold *Bloom, though, as I recall, the author of* The Closing of the American Mind *was more troubled by German than French diseases, thinking that anyone resistant to the former would be unlikely to go down with the latter. But I wonder if I can ask you to say a bit more concerning the state of higher education in the USA. Can things really have declined as far as you suggest?*

Yes, they certainly can. William Bowen and Derek Bok, former presidents of Princeton and Harvard respectively, have just published a book whose subtitle (the most truly descriptive one) is, *Long-Term Consequences of Considering Race in College and University Admissions*. There are other important books on the same topic, which even the White House and Congress recognize as an urgent problem. Not long ago there was a referendum in San Francisco about whether to offer school children courses in what was briefly known as 'Ebonics'. This is a cant word, meant to dignify black street vernacular. Now no doubt our spoken language is in a constant state of change and development, and it would be a mistake to try rigidly to confine and codify it. Nevertheless, legitimizing 'Ebonics' would make a hash of spelling, grammar and syntax. In the eastern part of the country many quite well-educated Haitians have settled, who are well-spoken and bilingual. Their status even within the black community is respected, and this has led a lot of less educated mothers to name their sons 'Antwan'. Not long ago a name cropped up regularly in the Washington papers of a young black man involved in drug crimes. He was named Rayful Edmunds. My wife and I puzzled about that name for quite a while until she figured out that his first name was supposed to be Raphael. Clearly people who think and write thus are somehow eager to have it both ways: they want the right to use biblical or foreign names and words, but they also want the right to spell them any way they choose.

And this is but the beginning of the problem. Let me adduce some personal experiences at the university level. Many universities are concerned, both for legitimate reasons as well as for the sake of appearances, to admit minorities on a special (i.e. not wholly academic) basis. It is a form of 'affirmative action', aimed at diversifying the student body, and on the face of it, ethically irreproachable. What comes to pass in actual fact is that astonishingly unqualified students – not always black ones – are admitted to the university; the admissions office and the administration glow and gleam in the generous rectitude of these policies, and the faculty are left to provide what amounts to emergency care for the intellectually undernourished – which in turn means that many classes and courses must be taught at a remedial level, a matter from which administrators turn away like Pontius Pilate, washing their hands of the matter. And some teachers, in despair, decide simply to ignore these elementary matters, not taking them into account with regard to their grading practices.

I can give you some idea of the problem as I encountered it. You may remember Arnold reporting, in 'Literature and Science', 'I once mentioned in a school-report, how a young man in one of our English training colleges having to paraphrase the passage in *Macbeth* beginning,

Can'st thou not minister to a mind diseased?

turned this line into, "Can you not wait upon the lunatic?"' Well, imagine poor Arnold's distress if he found that by way of paraphrasing the following lines from a sonnet by Hopkins,

Generations have trod, have trod, have trod;
And all is seared with trade; bleared, smeared with
    toil;
And wears man's smudge and shares man's smell:
    the soil
Is bare now, nor can foot feel, being shod

a student would one day write, 'Man, however, is insensitive to his own destruction because he is wearing shoes.' That was not composed by a black student, nor were the following observations:

> 'Because of limitations and setbacks of technology during the Elizabethan period, Shakespeare, as well as his writing contemporaries, was left with the responsibility of presenting the main theme and emotion of a dramatic work through the words of his characters.'

> 'The concern which is held about the briefness of life tends to be doing so because of their focus on its end.'

> 'The reader almost gets a warm feeling from reading the first stanza.'

And finally, almost sublimely,

> 'Each of these objects are used in an extremely opposite manner than that which they were originally devised.'

All these passages were turned in by my own students, the final one by a senior English major in the fall term of 1984. What this means is that the student had taken enough courses in the English department to qualify as a major, and this meant a good number of courses in various periods. It clearly also meant that my distinguished colleagues had taken no notice whatever of the student's limitations, a matter I was able to confirm by discovering her grades in the other English courses she took, which were uniformly high. Consider, if you will, what this made me think of my colleagues.

How do you react to those who say that every generation throws up people who claim that the higher education system is in crisis? The idea that it has been all but destroyed by moral and philosophical relativism did not originate in The Closing of the American Mind, *after all. It was to be found in Mortimer Adler and Robert Hutchins's* The Higher Learning in America, *which had been published over fifty years earlier. And Hutchins, it's maybe worth adding, had gone on pressing the charge throughout the '40s and '50s, declaring, at about the time you were embarking on your own university career, that the universities had become 'high-class flophouses where parents send their children to keep them off*

86

the labour market and out of their own hair.'

I have no 'solution' to the problem. Ignorance, incompetence, like the poor, are always with us. As to the value of a university education, if I remember correctly, in Huxley's *After Many a Summer Dies the Swan,* there was a millionaire who would only hire Ph.Ds to pump gas at his service stations; and the value of those degrees has only diminished since that novel was published.

I'd like to go back to that quotation of Harold Bloom's for a moment. It's from The Best of the Best American Poetry 1988—1997, *an anthology he edited, which not only makes no space for any of the poems included by Adrienne Rich in* The Best American Poetry 1996, *but also denounces that book with a Leavis-like ferocity. Indeed, 'denounces' is too weak a word. Better would be 'anathematizes': 'That 1996 anthology ... seems to me a monumental representation of the enemies of the aesthetic who are in the act of overwhelming us. It is of a badness not to be believed, because it follows the criteria now operative: what matters most are the race, gender, sexual orientation, ethnic origin, and political purpose of the would-be poet. I ardently wish that I were being hyperbolical, but in fact I am exercising restraint ... Bursting with sincerity, the 1996 volume is a Stuffed Owl of bad verse, and of much badness that is neither verse nor prose ...' The Spartans are taking no prisoners, obviously!*

I'm not sure what you're asking me – is it whether I share Bloom's ferocity or simply the grounds of his displeasure? Certainly I share the grounds and premises of his repudiations. They apply, alas, not exclusively to any anthology such as Rich's, but to a pervasive condition in American letters. I can see it in the politics of this year's National Book Awards, the winner of which is due to be named well before this interview sees print. Already made public are the names of the five leading candidates for a prize supposedly bestowed for the best book of poetry of the year. Absent from the list are the names of Mark Strand, W.S. Merwin, Brad Leithauser, Nicholas Christopher, Edward Hirsch and J.D. McClatchy. That not one of these even made the list of contenders speaks volumes.

One of the things you produced in the '80s was an edition of George Herbert's poetry, The Essential Herbert. *How big an undertaking was this?*

The editing of the Herbert volume was no great editorial task, since I relied entirely on the authority of the text as established by Hutchinson in the Clarendon edition. My contribution, such as it was, confined itself to a brief introduction, and a few innovative notes. (There are a few more I wish I were able to add, but the publisher does not want to change the format for a few alterations. For example, in Herbert's 'Dotage', the phrase 'Nothing between two dishes' is glossed by Hutchinson as 'A Spanish proverb.' This is a mistake, or at least I can add that the phrase derives from a distinctly Italian method of cooking such dishes as *pesce o carne tra i due piatti*, and can be found in Marcella Hazan's *More Classic Italian Cooking*. To be sure, Hazan has no recipes for cooking 'nothing'; the fish or meat of the recipe is placed between two plates, the upper one turned upside down, the lower one heated, and the food is steamed in its own vaporized juices. There are a few other discoveries about isolated details in the Herbert poems I am pleased to have made.)

A recent issue of The Formalist, *a journal on which you and Richard Wilbur serve as advisers, reprints an interesting piece by him entitled 'Traditional Verse Forms'. I'd like to quote from it, and at some length, if I may:*

> *'Let me say a little about those traditional verse forms which were bequeathed to us by the masters — by those whom Yeats addresses as 'sages standing in God's holy fire.' When a formal poet feels a poem coming on, he reaches into the toolbox of traditional means and picks out a meter which seems likely to suit his hazily emerging thought; he tentatively decides whether the services of rhyme will be needed; he tries to foresee whether the argument of his poem will want to be paragraphed into stanzas; and then he gets going — knowing, of course, that as his poem finds its voice he may change his mind about what devices will further it. Many formal poems, nowadays, are constructed in that ad hoc fashion, and they sometimes arrive at rhyme schemes and stanza patterns which are quite without precedent or name. On the other hand, the poet has a splendid resource in all those tested verse-forms which have been handed down to us: the couplet, the canzone, the Spenserian stanza, the rondeau, the sonnet, and so on. These various structures have something of that benign, enabling character which I ascribed to good manners, but with the difference that they are all optional, and should only be used*

when they are peculiarly appropriate to some incipient ut-
terance. Robert Frost once said something like this: that if
you feel like saying something for about eight lines, and
then qualifying or unsaying it for six lines or so, you are
probably about to write a Petrarchan sonnet. That is the
way it should happen: the beginning poem, as it material-
izes, should choose that form whose logic will provide it
with precision, economy and power.'

Is this a view with which you're in complete agreement? If not, can you
say where you dissent?

I'd go along with Wilbur and Frost as far as they go, though there's much
more to be said about 'received forms'. For example, some of them are
certainly more demanding than others, and while Frost's easy description
of the practical value of the Petrarchan sonnet form is plausible in its way,
it might be more difficult to show how a mode of thought would 'natu-
rally' fall into the form of a villanelle or a sestina. Sometimes an estab-
lished, traditional form is taken on because it is a challenge; sometimes
because the form itself suggests the tone or attitude of a period — as
when the sonnet was once confined almost exclusively to the topic of
love, so that when one saw a fourteen-line poem (or, in the case of *Romeo
and Juliet*, heard the two young lovers, upon their first meeting and speak-
ing to one another, utter antiphonal quatrains in three exchanges, fol-
lowed by a couplet, one knew that love was being uttered in an estab-
lished form that even the unprepared ear could detect while sitting, or
standing, in the audience.) Frost himself knew of this traditional link of
form to content, dating back to the earliest sonneteers of the late middle
ages, well enough so that in his superb sonnet, 'The Silken Tent', he uses
imagery drawn, it would almost seem, from the unicorn tapestries at Cluny,
at least as regards the design of the tent itself; and its silken material as-
sures us that this is not some casual pup-tent. In the same way, there was
a passage in the original draft of *The Waste Land* composed not merely in
Popean couplets, but in which Eliot pointedly rhymed 'tray' with 'tea,' a
rhyme Pope would have found quite in accordance with his own lines,
'Here thou, great Anna! whom three realms obey, / Dost sometimes coun-
sel take — and sometimes Tea.' By deliberately imitating Pope's kind and
style of writing couplets (distinct from the ways they were used by Brown-
ing or Yeats, for example) Eliot hoped to catch something of the spirit of
eighteenth-century satiric verse devoted to social topics such as are mocked
in *The Rape of the Lock*. Having raised the name of Eliot, his work affords

some further possibilities as regards received forms, for he was an ingenious innovator with such forms. In *Four Quartets* he created what was an utterly original form of the sestina, in which the corresponding lines of each of the six stanzas rhyme with one another — and yet the poem is easily identified as a sestina. He also made innovations in the *terza rima* form by alternating masculine and feminine endings, instead of rhyming. In these cases, traditional forms have led the poet into creative experiments that have served him very well. As for sestinas, commonly they are written in pentameter lines, in order to place a convenient distance between the terminal words, and thus give the poet a decent space for invention that will make the sequence of those words appear to fall into place in some natural and pertinent order. When Elizabeth Bishop daringly writes her poem entitled 'Sestina' in tetrameters, we cannot fail to admire the enormous skill and deftness with which she carries off the task imposed by the form itself. Donald Justice has performed the same feat in a couple of sestinas. While these are all sestinas, they are also adventurous variations on the form. What troubles me in Wilbur's comment is his, as I think, Frostian assertion: 'That is the way it should happen.' This is prescriptive, and in this it resembles Frost's *ars poetica*, 'The Figure a Poem Makes', which sets out the solitary way a poem must find its path into the poet's mind and onto his page. Frost rejects any poem not composed according to his method. And it's clear that his method would not have worked for many poets. I have explained my dissent from Frost's views in the Preface to my Mellon Lectures.

There's a poem of yours I'd like to ask you about here. It's called 'Terms', and is a variety of sestina. However, unlike the traditional sestina, which employs six six-line stanzas, a three-line envoy, and six terminal words, 'Terms' employs five twelve-line stanzas, a five-line envoy and just five terminal words. Moreover, the order in which these terminal words appear is a deal more complicated than it is in the standard sestina, with the first stanza patterned 1, 2, 1, 1, 3, 1, 1, 4, 4, 1, 5, 5, the next five patterned in accordance with a formula stipulating replacement of a 1 with a 5, a 2 with a 1, a 3 with a 2, a 4 with a 3, and a 5 with a 4, and the envoy patterned 1, 2, 4, 5, 3. Dante employed the form in his 'Amor, tu vedi ben che questa donna'; it was revived by Auden, who used it in his 'Canzone', and it was used again by Merrill in 'Samos'. What attracted you to it, I wonder? Was it simply the technical challenge?

Well, yes. It was the technical challenge. Dante said, after writing his (he

may, for all I know, have invented the form himself) that in composing
the poem he was loading himself with chains, and that, having written
one such poem, he would never write another. And he didn't. Up until a
few days ago I would confidently have said that I knew of no one who
had written two of them. But then I received in the mail a superb poem in
this form, written by a man who had sent me an excellent one some years
before. His name is Agha Shahid Ali, and he lives in Northampton, Mas-
sachusetts. He must be entitled to some sort of entry in *The Guinness
Book of Records*. Yes, Auden revived the form, and it is to him that new
attempts at it owe the new life it has enjoyed in our times. Not only Mer-
rill but John Hollander, Marilyn Hacker, L.E. Sissman, all have ventured
to load themselves with the chains Dante had forged. I can't think of any
other verse form that so suddenly disappeared and was so suddenly re-
vived. Moreover, the writing of one, as anyone who has attempted it
knows, calls into question the views of Wilbur and Frost you just men-
tioned.

Well, it was partly for this reason that I asked you about it.

Such a form demands an enormous amount of preliminary strategy, from
the choice of the terminal words to the decision of how the trajectory of
the poem will be governed by the fact that in any given stanza, one of the
terminal words will firmly predominate, appearing as it must six times. So
it is important, when planning the poem, to give that word the promi-
nence it deserves or needs at the right point as the poem draws to a close.
I made a couple of false starts at the one I wrote, precisely because I had
not made the right allowance for this kind of concentration on the right
word in the terminal stanza.

*I'd like to ask you a few questions about 'Meditation', to which you've
attached another unidentified epigraph, this time from Yeats's 'Under
Ben Bulben'. First, I'd like you to satisfy my curiosity about the third and
final section of the poem. Is it a real painting you describe there, or is this
what John Hollander would call a* notional ecphrasis, *rather than an ac-
tual one?*

The answer is that this is a painting of my own making, with de-
tails borrowed from great altarpieces by the likes of Giovanni Bellini
and Cima da Conegliano. There are a number of these stunning works in
Venice, and I have assembled my own composition out of them, pretty

much *ad lib.*

My second, and more important, question has to do with the poem's argument. While it seems to me that I understand what is going on in each of the three sections, and see the links between them, still I don't grasp the poem as a whole. At the risk of sounding glib, my experience of the poem is rather like the experience you describe in its opening section, where the separate instruments can be discerned, but not their conversation. Is there anything you can say that might help me? Or have you enough sympathy for that view of Valéry's, according to which everything that counts is well-veiled — you have called the paragraph in which that comment occurs 'astute' — to want to resist the question?

I've attempted to answer this elsewhere, so I hope you will allow me to quote myself. This comes from a comment on the poem that appears in David Lehman's anthology, *Ecstatic Occasions, Expedient Forms*. Of my poem I remark there: 'It's based on a set of metaphors or figures that are acoustical or auditory in character, and that move from music and its opposite, cacophony, to an articulate silence; that is, from a perilous oscillation between the real world and an imagined one; or rather, not oscillation but interpenetration. The imagined world is art, whether as music or painting. But it is a world into which we enter, and even seem to inhabit, however briefly. The poem in its three parts is about the strange way we negotiate our entrance into this world, and the strangeness of that world in which all disharmonies are somehow reconciled. "'Facts'," wrote Kenneth Clark in *Landscape into Art*, "become art through love ... Bellini's landscapes are the supreme instance of facts transfigured through love."' I would add now that the world in which 'all disharmonies are somehow reconciled' is what Keats was writing about in the letter cited earlier, regarding *King Lear*. Anyway, I was not trying to be obscure but to write about something that in the end is really quite mysterious: how art can somehow include the sordors and anguishes of life and yet accommodate them in some utterly benign and satisfying pattern.

I'm intrigued by 'Meditation"s echoes of 'What the Thunder Said'. How deliberate was this?

Yes, you're right. Isn't it curious that one has only to begin two consecutive pentameter lines with the words 'After the' for an alert reader to say: 'Ha! Eliot! The Waste Land. 'What the Thunder Said.' It's an index of the authority and durability and resonance of his words. And yet I think this echo, if that's what it is, was quite unconscious, a faint reminiscence of a familiar music ('That strain again') buried obscurely in the back of my mind. The general tenor of my lines is really unlike Eliot's. Mine are vaguely hopeful, and at least gentle, whereas his are agonized and full of despair.

If Yeats still ranks highest in your twentieth century pantheon, where does Eliot come, I wonder? You'd echoed him in earlier poems, of course ...

His influence on me was not merely formidable, but so strong that I had consciously to try to erase it to some extent. Naturally, it was the influence both of his poetry and his criticism, though far more of his poetry than of his criticism. So let's talk about the latter first. Certain of his essays had an astonishing and enduring effect on me. Not many of them, but a few. 'Tradition and the Individual Talent,' undeniably. The essays on the Metaphysicals and Marvell as well. The influence of these was both direct and indirect; by which I mean that apart from reading the essays themselves, many of my teachers had absorbed Eliot's views and made them more or less their own, passing them on to me when I was a student. One of these teachers, Austin Warren, was not far from being an acolyte of Eliot's, and was certainly a co-religionist. For him, Eliot's views were virtually sacred text. Eliot may not have been the only one to revive the Metaphysicals (Grierson went before, making straight the highway, and crying in the wilderness) but Eliot seems to have earned all the credit. In this he was (though he would scarcely have liked the comparison) like Felix Mendelssohn, who brought Bach back from an obscurity in which he had been lost for nearly one hundred years. Some of the other essays meant less to me, while others (including what he had to say about *Othello* and *Hamlet*) I seriously disagree with. The *Hamlet* essay, with its formulation about an 'objective correlative' is really about Eliot's own imaginative methods as a poet, rather than about Shakespeare. And in a curious way the two Milton essays are also perversely personal while parading under the guise of objective criticism. In the first, we are told that Milton is a dangerous and pernicious influence, and ought to be avoided; twenty-five years later, in his second Milton essay, he lifts his ban and allows us to resume reading *Paradise Lost*. Why the change? What has altered in the interval? Was he mistaken in imposing his condemnatory edict in the first place? Not on your life. Milton II begins by declaring that Eliot was right in banning Milton's influence at the time he did so, and right again in giving him clearance later on. There is something stiff and imperious about the way Eliot presents these views. His prose itself is infected by his rather pompous view of his own importance. I'm reminded of a passage in *Jude the Obscure* in which, defining the requisite qualities of a gentleman, Hardy declares 'but one must try not to sound like a bishop.' I'm aware of the irony of citing Hardy against Eliot, because in Eliot's rather infamous essays appearing under the title of *After Strange Gods*, he gives Hardy even shorter shrift than he gave Milton: 'In consequence of his self-absorption, he makes a great deal of landscape; for landscape is a passive creature which lends itself to an author's mood. Landscape is fitted too for the purposes of an author who is not interested at all in men's minds, but only in their emotions. It is only, indeed, in their emotional paroxysms that most of Hardy's characters come alive. This emotionalism seems to me to be a symptom of decadence; it is a cardinal point of faith in the romantic age, to believe that there is something admirable in violent emotion for its own sake, whatever the emotion or whatever the object. But it is by no means self-evident that human beings are most real when most violently excited; ...' These strictures of Eliot's are directed at Hardy's fiction, of course, but he would presumably have had to direct them at the poetry too, had he ever written about it, because that just as surely makes use of landscape, and just as surely involves strong emotion. The attitude is difficult to understand, and for a variety of reasons. Consider first the disdain for landscapes. How many other poets would be affected by Eliot's anathema? Wordsworth would be one; and Frost would be another; but it's worth pointing out that Eliot himself would not be unaffected. A short while back, I got a letter from a friend, David Havird, in Louisiana, who visited England recently, and Hardy country in particular. The first part of what he says about this trip isn't directly relevant to what I want to say about Eliot, but I'll include it anyway, because it sets the scene, and is quite amusing: 'In Dorset we made a pilgrimage to Hardy's grave, in the Stinsford Churchyard, near Dorchester. Rather, I should say the grave of Hardy's heart. "Here lies the heart of Thomas Hardy, O.M." – this across the front of a whitish slab that's shaped like the top of a casket. Along either side of this slab are inscriptions that record that this is also the burial place of Hardy's two wives: it would appear that his heart is nestled between the two of them. The story goes that when Hardy died, a couple of his friends petitioned the Prime Minister for permission to have him interred in Westminster Abbey. This permission was immediately granted – to the dismay of Hardy's widow and sister, who wished to honour Hardy's request that he be buried in the churchyard which held the bones of his mother and father. So, a compromise was struck. A surgeon was to remove the heart for burial there; the body would be cremated and the ashes interred in London. This I knew from the biographies. (Hardy was the subject of my dissertation.) What I had never heard was this: the surgeon did remove the heart, wrapped it in a towel, and placed it in a cookie tin. But when the undertaker came to retrieve it, there was no heart, but sitting nearby was a very satisfied looking cat. So, the cat was killed and buried in the Stinsford Churchyard. Whether true or not, Hardy would have appreciated the story ...' And now I come to the part of my friend's letter which is relevant to Eliot and those disparaging remarks about landscape. After visiting Stinsford Churchyard, he went on to visit East Coker, the village which gave its name to the second of Eliot's *Four Quartets*: 'It had never occurred to me to look up East Coker on the map, but there it was in Hardy Country – and why not? You read the opening lines of "East Coker" and enter the world of Hardy's novels.'

Hardy has had the last word, I suspect, like the landscape described in The Return of the Native, *'slighted and enduring'.*

Indeed.

And what of Eliot's other stricture, the one against emotionalism?

Eliot seems astonishingly unaware that Hardy's aim – and this is true of the poetry as well as the fiction – was the creation of something containing the elements of the *tragic*, as we have come to understand this from classical Greek examples. And this means, as it meant to Sophocles and Euripides, the presentation of people in states of crisis. The grandeur, the terror and the pity Hardy hopes to engender is intended to be recognized as kin to and derived from the great Greek tragedians.

As I said, this criticism of Hardy was set out in *After Strange Gods*, which is perhaps better known for being the volume containing Eliot's interdiction of what he called 'free-thinking Jews' from what he thought of as an ideal community, going on to say, 'And a spirit of excessive tolerance is to be deprecated.' What appals about this is that the book appeared in 1934 (though the lectures themselves were delivered in 1933), when some of the most brutal acts against Jews in Germany were commonly reported in the public press. It took a kind of strange insensitivity and self-absorption to utter these views before an audience at the University of Virginia in those days of early Nazism without any sense of embarrassment. The embarrassment must have come later, because he forbade the book to be reprinted, and it's now a rare item. This may have been

Eliot's first prose assault on 'free-thinking Jews' (from which group he must have mentally excluded Spinoza, whom he seems to have admired), but it was not the last. As Ronald Bush reports, as editor of the *Criterion*, 'Eliot chose to print an unsigned review' in 1936 of a book calling attention to the plight of German Jews, and urging action in their behalf. The book was called *The Yellow Spot: The Outlawing of Half a Million Human Beings*. It was composed by a committee of 'investigators', and contained an introduction by the Bishop of Durham. Read today, in the hindsight of the Holocaust's hideous thermal glow, the review is utterly shocking in its cold dismissiveness, even of the Bishop of Durham. Bush, like many others, believed that Eliot wrote the review, as he apparently wrote a good number of such unsigned reviews for the *Criterion*. But after his death, in a letter to the *TLS*, Valerie Eliot wrote to say the review was written by Montgomery Belgion. This may indeed be true, though it doesn't seem much to matter. Eliot, as editor, published it, when he was perfectly free to omit it.

Christopher Ricks quotes that review in T.S. Eliot and Prejudice, and hits the nail squarely on the head, twice, describing the piece as 'armoured in fastidious unimagination,' and accusing its author of 'cruelly self-right-eous impercipience.'

I am glad you mention Christopher Ricks, because in my view he addresses the explosive subject of Eliot's attitude to the Jews with greater subtlety, acuity and sensitivity than anyone else, though Anthony Julius's *T.S. Eliot, anti-Semitism and Literary Form* is perhaps more exhaustive than *T.S. Eliot and Prejudice*. But I was about to quote Katherine Anne Porter. Addressing the fact that the Bishop of Wakefield wrote in the papers that he had burned his copy of Hardy's *Jude The Obscure*, she commented, 'Of all evil emotions generated in the snake-pit of human nature, theological hatred is perhaps the most savage, being based on intellectual concepts and disguised in the highest spiritual motives.' Late in his life Eliot denied that he was anti-Semitic, and, as though this were proof, declared that his religious faith itself prohibited it.

He must have been feeling pretty desperate, to grasp at that particular straw.

I have this on the authority of Robert Giroux, who reported in *The Washington Post's Book World* of December 18th 1988 that, in a reply to a question from the Rev. William Turner Levy about the charge of anti-

Semitism, Eliot said: 'I am grieved and sometimes angered by this matter. I am not an anti-Semite and never have been. It is a terrible slander on a man. And they do not know, as you and I do, that in the eyes of the Church to be anti-Semitic is a sin.'

Someone should have reminded him of what Péguy said – as a gentile, a Christian, a poet, and an outspoken critic of the anti-Semitism of his time, he's an especially apt person to quote in this context – 'No-one is as competent as the sinner in matters of Christianity. No-one, except the saint.'

Of course, Eliot also cultivated the, first epistolary, and later personal friendship with Groucho Marx, an act not unlike the revelations by Mary McCarthy and Robert Lowell of their own Jewish connections.

What are your feelings about Eliot's prose more generally?

In thinking of Eliot's prose in general, I confess that I don't find it a joy to read, and these feelings are not based on ideological grounds. Arnold is a far better, less crotchety prose writer, more humane and better balanced. Many of Eliot's essays, while nominally on literary subjects, have a not altogether concealed religious sub-text and urgency; the one on Baudelaire, for example. Yet every once in a while Eliot, almost parenthetically, will make a shrewd and persuasive observation like this: '... although we do not feel, after reading Campion, that we know the man, Campion, as we do feel after reading Herrick, yet on other grounds, because he is so much the more remarkable craftsman, I should myself rate Campion as a more important poet than Herrick, though very much below Herbert.' There is something compelling yet not obvious in this judgement, partly because not only is Herrick more detectably present in his poems than Campion, but so is Herbert, so the ranking of them appears to be irrelevant to the question of how much their personal presence is felt to inhabit their poems. But this is a matter Eliot himself felt equivocal about. Bush reports Eliot's dissatisfaction with 'Little Gidding' just after finishing it. He wrote to John Hayward, 'The defect of the whole, I feel, is the lack of some acute personal reminiscence (never to be explicated, of course, but to give power from well below the surface).' It looks as though considerations like this return us to the question you raised earlier about Snodgrass and Lowell and the personal details of their work, as distinct from my own.

And now to the poems. They are indisputably amazing. Strictly speaking (by which I mean, omitting *Practical Cats* and *The Inventions of the March Hare*) there are 52 poems that represent Eliot's entire poetic corpus. Even Ransom's frugal *Selected Poems* had 53; Hopkins had 76; Hart Crane 62; Hardy 947; Emily Dickinson 1,775. And all of these would be dwarfed by Browning or Tennyson. But almost every line of Eliot's poetry seems forged of the most durable steel, and while poems like 'Prufrock' or *The Waste Land* were mocked at or puzzled over at their first appearances, they are now, pretty much line for line, a part of our mental life, and are fixed in the memory of many of us. The careful skill of these poems, and of virtually all of Eliot's poems, is undeniable. And so, one is obliged to add with regret, is the malice of the earlier poems, up to perhaps 'Ash Wednesday'. There is contempt for the man Prufrock, for his vacillation, his wimpish lack of manliness. There is not much more sympathy for the poor, frustrated lady of the Jamesian titled 'Portrait of a Lady', or for the young man she is infatuated with. I've been told, on what authority I cannot say, that the distinguished critic John L. Sweeney admitted to his friends that he was deeply hurt by the whole sequence of Sweeney poems, including, of course, 'Sweeney Agonistes'. Eliot created in this character someone of striking crassness, vulgarity and brutality. A murderer. To whom he gives a distinctly Irish name. And names in Eliot count for a lot. The Irish of Eliot's Boston days were regarded as distinctly lower-class. Want ads for jobs often enough contained the subscript: *No Irish need apply*. As for the poems' Jews, they are more plentiful and at least equally unpleasant ...

Do you remember what Lowell said about the allegations that Eliot's early poetry was anti-Semitic? I'm thinking of the interview he gave Frederick Seidel for The Paris Review, *back in 1961.*

It's a curiously equivocal statement, isn't it? ' ... in Eliot, the Jew spelled with a small *j* in "Gerontion", is that anti-Semitism or not? Eliot's not anti-Semitic in any sense, but there is certainly a dislike of Jews in those early poems. Does he gain in the fierceness of writing his Jew with a small *j*? Very ugly emotions perhaps make a poem.' This is surely deeply muddled. How could Eliot not be anti-Semitic *in any sense* while successfully giving the impression to so many that he was, and requiring so many others to come to his defence? And of course there is something very odd about Lowell's confining his remarks to Eliot's use of the lower-case *j* for *Jew*, as though Bleistein did not show up, repulsively, in 'Burbank with a Baedeker: Bleistein with a Cigar,' and in the discarded passages of *The Waste Land* ...

And as though the woman in 'Sweeney Among the Nightingales' who 'Tears at the grapes with murderous paws' didn't happen to be called 'Rachel née Rabinovitch'.

Indeed.

I wonder if this wasn't Lowell struggling to avoid saying in public what he would have been much less reluctant to say in private? Because in that same stretch of the interview with Seidel he came out with an extraordinary defence of what he called Pound's 'bad' and 'terrible' beliefs – '... they made him more human and more to do with life, more to do with the times. They served him. Taking what interested him in these things gave a kind of realism and life to his poetry that it wouldn't have had otherwise' – and yet, five years earlier, he had written to Pound, saying that he wouldn't return to St. Elizabeth's unless he desisted from making anti-Semitic remarks, and, just a few months after the interview, he wrote to Alfred Kazin, saying that Pound's anti-Semitism was 'like the voice of a drunkard telling people in cars to drive through the pedestrians', something nothing *could excuse.*

That line you mentioned just now, the one about 'Rachel née Rabinovitch': it's a line that seems to me never to have been sufficiently scrutinized. Normally *née* prefaces the maiden name of a woman who has since adopted her husband's surname, or gone about changing her name legally for one purpose or another. In Eliot's poem it is odd to be told what her maiden name is, since we have no other surname behind which she might disguise herself, a disguise (if that's what it is) that would be seriously compromised by her given name 'Rachel'. There lurks, I fear, the possibility that Eliot intended us to hear the word *nez*. In fact, it might be argued that if this intention is eliminated, the line simply makes no sense.

But there is one small gloss I would like to add to the general commentary on 'Gerontion'. It is a kind of art-history note, and is offered in connection with the lines: 'My house is a decayed house, / And the jew squats on the window sill, the owner, ...' We must begin with Luke's gospel, which states unequivocally that Jesus was born 'in a manger'. In almost all the northern Renaissance paintings of the scene, as well as in our modern-day crèches, an attempt is made to emphasize the conspicuously humble, stockyard accommodations of the holy family. But curiously, in Italian painting during the Renaissance an interesting iconography was developed that varied from this slightly. Sometimes a manger-like hut was affixed to what looked like the ruins of a grand, classical structure; sometimes the manger was omitted altogether, and only the classical ruins left. It used to be assumed that the painters who so designed their nativities were, like the Renaissance humanists among whom they lived, and who were sometimes their patrons, enamoured of the majestic remnants of a classical civilization that had all too long lain unappreciated. And this may, to some extent, have been the case. But this combination of ruined palace and rough shed appears in Fra Angelico's *Adoration of the Magi*, right here in Washington, and in Botticelli's *Adoration* at the Uffizi, Botticelli's other *Adoration*, also in Washington, and countless others. And this ruined palace-rough shed combination served the same purpose as another iconographic detail that crops up in such pictures: the stump of a tree, sawed off near its root, but with a single branch growing from it. These were ways of representing the old dispensation and the new one. In volume II of *Modern Painters* Ruskin states quite plainly: 'The ruined house is the Jewish dispensation.' Eliot's speaker in 'Gerontion', like his speakers in 'A Song for Simeon' and 'The Journey of the Magi', feels himself, in the words of Arnold, 'Wandering between two worlds, one dead, / The other powerless to be born.' This was a feeling Eliot must have experienced during what might be thought of as his wandering in the wilderness, the period during which, while he had nominally embraced the doctrines of the Anglican Church, he felt he had not fully acknowledged to himself the burden and the grace of faith, so he was in a spiritual no-man's land. Much of his most important poetry reflects this condition.

There is one last thing I would like to say concerning Eliot's anti-Semitism. It concerns an aspect of his prejudice that, I believe, even Anthony Julius has not examined. Eliot wrote blurbs and endorsements of books he admired, a number of which, like Djuna Barnes's *Nightwood*, exhibit unembarrassed anti-Semitism. A number of such books, bearing Eliot's commendations, are now lost to mind; at least, I've forgotten their titles and their authors. But I remember being much struck by their bigoted contents at the time I read them.

Part V of The Transparent Man *contains a number of poems prompted by the deaths of people you'd known: David Kalstone, James Wright, L.E. Sissman, and, more obliquely, Flannery O'Connor. It also contains a traditional sestina I'd somehow overlooked until De Snodgrass drew it to my attention last summer. We were up late one night, talking about the difficulties a poet confronts when trying to write convincingly about evil, and De asked me if I knew 'The Book of Yolek'. I had to tell him I didn't, and assumed that he must have come across it in a magazine some-*

where. Next morning, when I came down to breakfast, I had a big sur-
prise, because there on the table was his copy of The Transparent Man,
with a marker at the pages I'd somehow missed. It's not often that a
poem raises the hair on the back of my neck, but it happened that morn-
ing. Like your much earlier poem, 'Rites and Ceremonies', it seems to me
one of the very best poems to have come out of the Holocaust. — Can I
ask you about its origins?

There were a number of sources: my having seen Flossenbürg was certainly
one. There was also a memorable photograph, one of the most famous to
survive from the Warsaw ghetto. It is of a small boy, perhaps five or six,
wearing a shabby peaked cap and short pants, his hands raised and a
bewildered, forlorn look on his face as he gazes off at something to the
side of the camera, while behind him uniformed, helmeted soldiers keep
their rifles trained on him, as one of them looks directly at the camera
without the least expression of embarrassment.

'To shame unvulnerable.'

But of course I did a lot of reading about the Holocaust. There were many
books, but one in particular proved helpful to me. It is an *Anthology of*
Holocaust Literature, and it's edited by Jacob Glatstein, Israel Knox, and
Samuel Margoshes. It contains, among other moving and terrifying, even
stomach-turning accounts, a piece by Hanna Mortkowicz-Olczakowa
which bears the title *Yanosz Korczak's Last Walk*. Yanosz Korczak was a
famous Jewish educator in Poland who, having been ordered to lead the
children of the orphanage where he taught to an assembly point from
which they would be taken to death camps, refused to part from them,
knowing, as they did not, where they were headed, and went with them
to their deaths. Among these children were 'little Hanka with the lung
trouble, Yolek who was ill ...' As you will notice, I recalled this account
imperfectly, and gave the bad lungs to Yolek instead of little Hanka. But
apart from such explicit sources, I found myself meditating on the sestina
form itself, without reference to any particular subject matter. I was think-
ing of how the various sestinas I knew operated. And it occurred to me
that, because of the persistent reiteration of those terminal words, over
and over in stanza after stanza, the sestina seemed to lend itself espe-
cially well to a topic felt obsessively, unremittingly. And when this reali-
zation fell into place with the other preoccupations aroused by my read-
ing and that remembered photograph, I had the materials of my poem.

'The Book of Yolek' has a German epigraph, which translates as 'We

have a law / And by that law he must die'. Can you tell me where that comes from?

The epigraph is Martin Luther's translation of John 19:7. It is also the text of one of the most stirring choruses in Bach's *St. John's Passion*.

I mentioned James Wright a moment ago. He's one of a number of American poets whose work is barely known in the U.K. How do you rate his importance, this many years since he died?

Dr. Johnson remarked somewhere that during a poet's life he is judged by his worst poems, and after he is dead by his best. In my view, Wright's poems as a whole are very uneven. But his best ones are nothing short of marvellous. These poems are deeply moving and richly eloquent. But Jim had a decidedly sentimental side, and a weakness for what I think of as cheap and easy transcendence. I can give you an idea of what I mean by quoting some of his prose, in this case about a poet he revered. At one time he studied with an Italian professor who taught German poetry at the University of Vienna. Wright describes sitting in an unheated classroom with a few old men, regarding the professor, whose name was Susini. 'He stood still, peering into the dusk where we sat. Then he read a poem called "Verfall", the first poem in Georg Trakl's *Die Dichtungen*. It was as though the sea had entered the class at the last moment. For this poem was not like any poem I had ever recognized: the poet, at a sign from the evening bells, followed the wings of birds that became a train of pious pilgrims who were continually vanishing into the clear autumn of distances; beyond the distances there were black horses leaping in red maple trees, in a world where seeing and hearing are not two actions, but one.' I submit that this is very soft and cumulo-nimbus-like prose. I don't have a copy of the Trakl poem, whose title means *Decay*, but Jim's account of it does not tempt me to go out and find it. He makes it sound like a rather dreamy painting by Chagall. From time to time his own poems yield to his taste for these facile transformations and casual epiphanies. But his really good poems are wonderful, and a solid part of the achievement of his generation of American poets. More than that, a handful of his poems are as durable and memorable as anything of our time that I can think of. He was also, though this is probably irrelevant to your question, an uncommonly *good* man. He was a loyal friend of my brother's, and he had one of the most retentive memories for poetry of anyone I've ever known.

I heard a nice story about Wright. He and another poet gave a reading at

Wayne State many years ago, and next day they had to rise at the crack of dawn in order to catch early flights home. Shortly after getting into the taxi, and without any warning, Wright's companion began to intone:

> *Yet once more, O ye Laurels, and once more*
> *Ye Myrtles brown, with Ivy never-sere,*
> *I com to pluck your Berries harsh and crude*
> *And with forc'd fingers rude,*
> *Shatter your leaves before the mellowing year ...*

And he didn't stop till he reached the poem's end, a hundred and ninety or so lines, and however many miles, later. This would have been re-markable enough, but what made it all the more remarkable was the fact that the whole performance was done in the voice of W.C. Fields! Appar-ently, Wright was so overwhelmed, he could do no more at the end than whisper, 'Thank-you.' I mention this in the hope that you might be able to cast light on the identity of the companion?

How absolutely astonishing that this story — rather embellished in transit — should have found its way to you in England. I must try to be as truthful as I can about this, labouring under the handicap of a faulty memory in my latter days. To be sure, the story is about me; I'm the guy who did 'Lycidas' in the voice of Fields. I have no memory whatever of the taxi ride, nor even, to my shame, of sharing a poetry-reading platform with Jim at Wayne State. That doesn't mean it didn't happen, but I recall noth-ing of the sort. And I can state with some conviction that I never had committed the whole of 'Lycidas' to memory. Large parts of it, yes. It was my habit to allow Fields a few interpolative comments now and again. I remember that after the lines

> He must not float upon his watery bier
> Unwept, and welter to the parching wind,
> Without the meed of some melodious tear

I would pause, and let Fields observe: 'That's very sad — that part about the watery beer.' Your account of Wright's quiet and generous 'Thank you' for my performance, while nothing I remember, is absolutely char-acteristic.

The story was related to me by De Snodgrass, who is pretty sure he had it from Wright himself (though he admits his memory is not what it was).

As a matter of fact, De didn't just relate it me, but acted it out as well, so that I now have the indelible picture of Snodgrass doing Wright doing Hecht doing Fields doing Milton!

I can give you another example of my incorrigible ways with great poetry. During the years I taught at Bard I gave a course in English poetry from, say, Skelton and Wyatt to Hopkins and Housman. It was a big class, something like forty to forty-five students, and I used to take their long mid-term and term papers back with me to my New York apartment for three-day weekends, where correcting and grading took up the whole time. I required my students to write papers that paid careful attention to important details of the poem they were assigned, and to quote the passages on which they commented. One time they had been assigned to write about Dryden's 'A Song for St. Cecilia's Day'. Now, when you sit down to read forty-five papers about a single poem it's not long before the poem's words tend to blur and become almost meaningless, to lapse into nonsense syllables. And I found that this was what was happening to Dryden's words in my mind as I read them over and over again in paper after paper. I knew that I had to find some way of restoring them to something like reality, in the mind and in the ear. And I found that I could do this if I read the lines in a cockney accent based on that of Stanley Holloway's in *My Fair Lady*. Thus we would have:

> From 'armony, from 'eav'nly 'armony
> This universal Frime began;
> When Niture underneath an 'eap
> Of jarring Atoms lie
> And could not 'eave 'er 'ead,
> The tuneful voice was 'eared on 'igh
> Harrise, ye more than dead.

This turned out to work very well, and was a great help with my papers. I was pleased enough to phone Auden, who was then living in New York, and render a few lines for his pleasure. And indeed he seemed to like them, and invited me to visit. But I had my hands full with my papers, and while I could have gone some other time, I never did.

Amongst contemporary novelists, whose books give you the greatest pleasure?

I would list Philip Roth, Stanley Elkin, William Maxwell, Saul Bellow,

Vladimir Nabokov.

What other kinds of reading do you like to do?

Biographies, history, art and architectural history, and what is sometimes called intellectual history, a form that covers a lot of ground.

Just how well-versed you are in art and architectural history will be obvious to anyone who's read your work, creative or critical. Do your remember how your passion for these things developed?

It began with a thick book of colour reproductions of art masterpieces, edited by Thomas Craven, which I used to pore over as a boy. I was brought up in New York City, and lived quite close to the Met, which I visited with increasing pleasure as I grew older. Europe, of course, was an education all by itself, and Rome in particular. I became entranced by the critical works of Gombrich, Panofsky, Wind and Wittkower, all that learned crowd at the Warburg Institute. As for architecture, Rome was of course a daily education, as were some architectural historians, architects and art critics through whose eyes I was richly and personally instructed. These included Frank Brown, William MacDonald, Irving and Marilyn Lavin, Robert Venturi and a number of others. My educational reading probably began with Geoffrey Scott, and spread in every direction.

Of contemporary artists and architects, whose work most appeals to you?

If I may be allowed to apply the word 'contemporary' in a generous and latitudinous way, I would list among the architects Mackintosh, Venturi, Pei, Kahn, Nervi, Saarinen. Among the painters and sculptors, Dimitri Hadzi, William Bailey, Milton Avery, Rothko, Pollock, Kandinsky, Matisse, Braque, Picasso and Baskin.

What non-literary interests do you have, apart from those you have already mentioned?

Music, travel and food. My wife, who is now an interior designer, wrote five cookbooks when we lived in Rochester. After our son was born, she wanted some occupation that would allow her to stay at home with the child, and be a useful and pleasant diversion. Since Rochester had no good restaurants, and since I loved her cooking, this seemed a happy decision for us both. My favourite among her books, *Cold Cuisine*, devoted to summer dishes that can be prepared in advance, contains, among its notes and acknowledgements, 'my husband, Tony, who ate this food all year without complaint; my son, Evan, who upholds the quality of my cuisine with fierce loyalty, although there are few things he will actually eat ...' In recent years we have tried to get to Italy for a couple of weeks every summer.

Were any of your poems ever set to music?

Yes. *The Seven Deadly Sins* has been set for tenor and piano by Robert Beaser. Leo Smit set a small group of songs, and I translated a text by Rilke that was set by Lukas Foss.

You left Rochester and went to Georgetown in 1985. What were your reasons for making the change?

During a two-year residence in Washington, when I held the post of Consultant in Poetry to the Library of Congress, a post now called the Poet Laureate, that wonderful, admirable man, Father Timothy Healy, who was president of Georgetown University, made honourable overtures to me by way of trying to persuade me to take up teaching duties at his university. We had met before, when he led a team of academics to evaluate the University of Rochester, where I was teaching, for some sort of accreditation. I was invited to meet him for cocktails at the home of the University Provost, and from the first we got on famously. He loved poetry, and was devoted to Donne. We went off with some others to dinner and everything about him seemed to my liking. So when he later made the invitation, I was very pleased. But other factors played their important part. As it happens, both my wife and I suffer from frost-bite. She got it from walking our son to kindergarten when she was not properly shod during a Rochester winter day. I got it in the army. As you may know, it's an irreversible condition, and so every winter we were in real pain. And there were other considerations, including the undeniable lure of the National Gallery of Art, the Phillips Collection, the Library of Congress, the Folger Shakespeare Library, too many other museums to mention, the beautifully landscaped public places, the dandy restaurants (Rochester had virtually none) which grew dandier and more numerous with time, and the comparatively easy accessibility to New York, by shuttle flight. We had and have many New York friends, and my publisher and editor is there.

You retired from teaching in 1993. Do you miss it at all?

Not in the least, and for reasons I think I must already have made clear. Though there is one other reason I can add. By the age of seventy, when I retired, my hearing had begun noticeably to deteriorate, and I found it increasingly difficult to hear students when they asked questions. It was humiliating to have to ask them to repeat what they had just asked, both for them and for me.

Since retiring, you've published The Hidden Law: The Poetry of W.H. Auden, *and* On the Laws of the Poetic Art, *your Andrew W. Mellon Lectures in the Fine Arts. While engaged on critical work of this kind, are you able to pursue your creative work too?*

The Auden book was composed while I was still teaching, and so were the Mellon Lectures. They were written during vacations and leaves of absence. In both cases, they took up time I might otherwise have tried to use for poems. I can't do both kinds of work at the same time.

What would a typical working day be like for you?

I like best to work in the mornings. I find my mind is both more alert, and, often, profitably the opposite. I mean that in the mildly and pleasantly dazed state I find myself in early in the day after rising — calm and without anxiety, still close to the comforts and suggestions of the world of sleep — I am near enough to unconscious sources, to essential memories, to feel I can call on buried resources for my poems. And once that state, largely passive, is over, my mind is at its most alert in the course of the day. I was once tactless enough to reply to some academic interviewer by shamelessly announcing that I liked to write and think in the mornings, and was content to teach in the afternoons when my mind was tired. My students were kind enough to be merely amused by this. I can go on working — at my own literary tasks, that is — until about mid-afternoon, when something in my metabolism slows me down, and I can no longer operate at full speed. I know this is not the case with everyone, and I've had colleagues who prefer to teach in the late afternoon or even the evening. Not for me.

I know you never use a word-processor, but what do you use, when writing poetry, and when writing prose?

I write poems longhand, and transcribe them to a typescript fairly soon, though not until many pencilled corrections and changes have already been made. I write prose directly on the typewriter, though I type so badly I often have to make a second draft. This must sound terribly old-fashioned and backwards of me, and perhaps it is. Nevertheless, I can remember being awed at viewing the *Collected Works and Letters* of Voltaire in the stacks of some library, and, again, seeing the *Collected Works* of John Ruskin, and realizing that both men wrote all they produced in longhand. And, if I remember correctly, Keats, whose letters are wonderful and many, made a 'fair copy' of each of his letters, regarding the first one as merely a draft.

Your most recent collection is Flight Among The Tombs, *which came out in 1996. The book is in two parts, the first of which,* The Presumptions of Death, *comprises twenty-two poems, to accompany twenty-two woodcuts by Leonard Baskin. What brought you together again, because you'd worked with him before, of course, most notably on* The Seven Deadly Sins.

It was Leonard who proposed joining forces again. We first became friends and collaborators when I was teaching at Smith in the late '50s, where he was also on the faculty. His remarkably handsome and intelligent wife, Esther, was dying of multiple sclerosis. When I first knew her she was ambulant and articulate; by the time I left, three years later, she was bedridden, needed nursing care around the clock, and had lost the power of speech. Leonard at that time had been at work on small sculptural figures of hanged men. But he was not wholly obsessed by death, and, being a printer as well as illustrator of fine books, he was then interested in emblem books, and wondered whether we might not do one together. *The Seven Deadly Sins* was a kind of preliminary foray along those lines. Then I left that part of the world, and poor Esther died; Leonard remarried in due course, and he and his wife settled in England for a while, where they saw a good deal of Ted Hughes. When Leonard returned to this country, he got in touch with me again. *The Presumptions of Death* was his proposal, and I was glad to fall in with it. Many of the 'characters' were proposed by him, including those in which Death speaks outright and undisguised. I proposed some of the 'characters' myself. The collection of poems and woodcuts, many of the latter in colour, were published by Baskin's Gehenna Press in a limited edition of sixty copies. The first ten are special — they contain an autograph copy of a poem by me, a drawing by Baskin, and a series of five hand-painted proofs — and are more expensive than the rest of the edition. The plain, ordinary run-of-the-mill copies for the drugstore trade are bound into marble paper over boards, with a leather inlay. The colophon is signed by poet and artist and all the woodcuts are signed and numbered. A copy goes for $7,500. Since then we've done another volume, same press, slightly smaller edition and slightly higher prices. It's called *A Gehenna Florilegium*, and its woodcuts of flowers are all in vivid colours. I'd better explain something about those prices. Leonard's work is well-known, and a collector's item for many institutions and individuals. Books like *Presumptions* and the *Florilegium* are sold through a subscription list, and there seem to be a good number of regular subscribers. The *Florilegium* presented a different problem for me from the earlier *Presumptions*. With the book about 'death' my central concern was to discover ways to achieve the widest variety of tone for the different poems. Nothing would have been easier than to fall into a routine mordancy, a weary, graveyard jocularity. I wanted the poems to sound as different from one another as possible. Hence, among other things, the variety of poetic forms. The challenge of the flower poems was different. First of all, the very idea of a collection of poems about flowers evokes a hideous nightmare of sentimental Victorian verses, with decorations by Walter Crane or Kate Greenaway. It was a matter of urgency to avoid anything of that sort. The 'flower poems' one thinks of that aren't tainted with this kind of maudlin sentimentality are such poems as Herrick's 'How Roses Came Red', 'How Violets Came Blue', 'To Daffodils' (a favourite of Frost's), which are charming in a period way, but not useful as models. And I had another motive on my agenda. It had been planned that in due course both poems and woodcuts of *The Presumptions of Death* would be issued in a trade volume by my regular publishers, and that the woodcuts would be printed in black and white. In the original Gehenna Press edition a good number of these woodcuts were in colour, but they were able to stand up pretty well without this feature. But clearly you cannot reproduce colourless woodcuts of flowers without the images suffering a great loss. I realized that my trade publishers would never be able to afford to print Baskin's flowers in colour; and this meant that when my poems eventually appear in a trade edition they will have to do so unaccompanied by any of Baskin's work. The poems, therefore, had to be so composed as to be manifestly independent of the images they were designed to accompany. And I believe I've written them so that the 'flower' element enters into them in a sly, indirect and often marginal way, and assembled without illustrations, they don't actually seem to be 'flower poems' at all.

In some of the Presumptions, *Death speaks* in propria persona, *just as he* had done in your early poem, 'Tarantula or The Dance of Death'. In others, he speaks as one of a range of characters — a punchinello, a film director, an archbishop, a carnival barker — danse macabre style. The poem I'm most affected by is the one in which Death speaks as a whore. It's the longest poem in the sequence, and bears comparison with some of your earlier monologues — 'The Grapes', for example. Its closing couplet has the same, completely disorienting, effect on me as certain lines of Rilke's. – Where does a poem like this come from? Do you know?

This will require a long answer, and one that will probably not be altogether satisfactory. Which, to answer your question briefly, is to say that I don't entirely know. Let me try to get out of this pickle by quoting Eliot — from his 'Conclusion' to *The Use of Poetry and the Use of Criticism*. This passage is pretty well-known. 'Why, for all of us, out of all that we have heard, seen, felt, in a lifetime, do certain images recur, charged with emotion, rather than others? The song of one bird, the leap of one fish, at a particular place and time, the scent of one flower, an old woman on a German mountain path, six ruffians seen through an open window playing cards at night at a small French railway junction where there was a watermill: such memories may have symbolic value, but of what we cannot tell, for they come to represent the depths of feeling into which we cannot peer.' This may come close to explaining some persistent images of bleak landscapes and scenes of desolation ('A Hill', 'An Autumnal', parts of 'See Naples and Die', of 'The Short End' and so forth) that find their way into my poems. The image of smoke rising straight up from woodlands on a windless, overcast winter day is something that has settled somewhere deep inside me, and, to paraphrase Eliot, means more to me than I can say.

So much for that. Now to a different and larger topic. I've known three women who committed suicide. Two of them are well-known: Sylvia Plath and Anne Sexton. The third I will call Mary. Apart from this spectacular inclination to self-destruction, one would suppose they had not much in common psychologically; and indeed they were very different from one another. I'm sure that psychiatrists would tell you that each person who is driven to suicide suffers from problems that are unique to that particular person, and no generalizations whatever can be drawn. Our mental worlds are as unique to us as F.H. Bradley said they were. Still and all, I can't help feeling, purely as an outside observer, that there was a strange link among these three women, in regard to the way they thought about the act of suicide itself. They were all intrigued by what we might call the 'lure', the 'audacity', what to at least two of them might fairly be called the 'glamour' of the act. Let me begin with some lines from Plath's 'Lady Lazarus':

> I have done it again.
> One year in every ten
> I manage it ——
> ....
> I am only thirty.
> And like the cat I have nine times to die.
>
> This is Number Three.
> ....
>
> Dying
> Is an art, like everything else.
> I do it exceptionally well.

With all allowances for the corrosive irony that this poem exhibits (in which she will go on to imagine herself as the resurrected, vengeful and retributive victim of concentration camp annihilation), I can't help feeling that the poem begins with an admission that death has its attractions, even if they consist of the chance to come back and destroy others. (And of course, to revert to psychiatric wisdom, suicide is medically regarded as an ultimate act of aggression.) Without wishing to labour the point any further, let me turn to some lines by Anne Sexton, these from a poem called 'Sylvia's Death':

> Thief! —
> how did you crawl into,
> crawl down alone
> into the death I wanted so badly and so long,
> ....
> the death we drank to

And it seems to be a matter of record that they did indeed 'drink' to the earlier attempted suicides in their careers. In the interview she gave *The Paris Review*, Sexton recalled going with Plath to the Ritz Bar in Boston, accompanied by George Starbuck. This was after class sessions with Lowell at Boston University: 'Sylvia and I would talk at length about our first suicides, in detail and depth – between the free potato chips. Suicide is, after all, the opposite of the poem. Sylvia and I often talked opposites. We talked death with a burned-up intensity, both of us drawn to it like moths to an electric lightbulb, sucking on it. She told the story of her first suicide in sweet and loving detail, and her description in *The Bell Jar* is just the same story. I wonder if we didn't depress George with our egocentricity; instead, I think, we three were stimulated by it – even George – as if death made each of us a little more real at the moment.'

Isn't it interesting that, just as Plath wrote of having died three times already, so Sexton talks of their suicides rather than their suicide attempts?

The locution is odd, but it is also characteristic. This is the way both Plath and Sexton spoke of these things, suggesting that they were entranced by flirtations with death, had passed over into its realm, and returned – like Lazarus. – To be sure, their poems are very different from one another's. Plath's poetry is one of cultivation, savagery and outrage, while Sexton's is Grand Guignol, with a defiantly cheerful vulgarity. (Reporting in *The Observer* for 16 July, 1967, regarding *Poetry International*, Mary Holland commented, 'Auden brooded in dark glasses while an American poetess went on and on about her "second suicide".' It was perfectly clear who was being referred to.) Even so, for both of them death was a sort of goal, and so it was for Mary, who was not a poet. But she was smitten by the glamour of both of them, and their suicide attempts were a part of that glamour she found attractive, and understood because she had made the attempt herself. When, after Sylvia's death, Mary found out that I not only had known her but knew Anne, who was still living, and whom I continued to see from time to time, Mary was unashamedly importunate, begging me to introduce her. I lived in New York at this time, and Anne just outside of Boston; I never went up there in those days, and she rarely came to New York because she had a Boston publisher, Houghton Mifflin. Nevertheless, an occasional reading would bring her my way, and once she let me know that she would be coming to the city with her designated biographer, Lois Ames, whom she had inherited from, of all people, Sylvia Plath. When Mary learned that Anne was to come to the city she implored me more desperately than ever to contrive an introduction, and so I arranged to take the three ladies to dinner at a nice French restaurant, rather an extravagance for me, and in more ways than one, since the evening turned into a minor disaster. Mary and I arrived first at the restaurant and were seated when Anne and Lois showed up. Though I had carefully explained to Anne that Mary had begged to meet her, and that the dinner was planned with that meeting in mind, Anne, who could be temperamental, chose to be so that evening. She took little if any notice of Mary, and made it clear that she was put out to have my exclusive attention to her compromised by the presence of an intruder. She proceeded to get very drunk. She may well have had a couple of drinks before she turned up at the restaurant, and while I can't remember anything about what we ate or drank that evening, it would have been normal for us to have had a cocktail, probably a martini, before ordering dinner and wine. Anyway, by mid-meal Anne was behaving erratically, and people at other tables were beginning to notice. At one point she fell right off her chair and onto the floor. Something about the way this happened suggested that some energy or effort on her part had gone into the fall. I had to get her up off the floor, usher her outside onto the dark city street, where the winter air, flaked with a light snow, seemed slowly to cool her down or sober her up, and we were able to make our way back to the table and finish our meal. Later, after the whole embarrassing evening was over, I apologized to Mary for Anne's very bad behaviour, and, to my astonishment, Mary not only felt that no apology was called for but found Anne even more enchanting than she had before. It was something about Anne's wilfulness, her reckless disregard of correct social behaviour, that she liked, and that had in her mind some obscure connection with the socially defiant act of suicide. She also had other heroines, social misfits and drug addicts. So I was not surprised to learn years later that she had killed herself.

These are some of the materials that went into the poem. Much of it, of course, was invented. The childhood game is indeed something I recall from my own childhood; the smoke of the last line is a conflation of the smoke of Sylvia's death camp, the death camp I saw myself, the ordinary funeral parlour crematorium and the smoke of an autumnal day mentioned in the opening lines. The speaker in my poem is not really at all like Mary, except insofar as they both were lured by the act of self-destruction. Almost all the particulars are different. But Sylvia, Anne and Mary all went into the poem in some way.

There's an old Zen technique for dealing with pain, which involves giving the sensation one's undivided attention. By turning it into an object of inquiry, it is said, one can deprive the sensation of its hurtfulness. I wonder if there isn't a sense in which this is what you're doing in The Presumptions of Death, *trying to draw death's sting by squaring up to him in all these different guises? If so, then by the time we get to the book's second part,* Proust on Skates, *and death has claimed two more of your friends — James Merrill and Joseph Brodsky — we are able to see in the magnificent elegies you write for them just how limited in its effec-*

tiveness the technique has been. Their deaths obviously hit you very hard …

I have no knowledge of the Zen techniques you speak of, and that one seems to me especially forbidding, like immersing oneself in the destructive element, or Mithridates habituating himself to poison by ingesting it. In any case, it does not apply to the writing of at least some elegies, including my own. The task of writing a poem is a difficult one for the likes of me, and few of them come easily. Writing is utterly preoccupying, and it not only leaves no room, in the course of composition, for grief, but it does nothing either to dispel or to indulge such grief. The motives of an elegy are, first, to make a good poem, and then to make it a tribute to someone in particular. And there may be a hidden, Miltonic motive: 'So may some gentle Muse / With lucky words favour my destined urn, / And as he passes turn, / And bid fair peace be to my sable shroud.'

Well, it was the Presumptions *I had in mind when I mentioned that Zen technique, not the elegies. But that said, you're quite right to criticize my naïve reading of the latter, treating them like – to revert to the imagery you introduced earlier in our discussion – seismography of the soul.*

But to turn to your question about the deaths of Jimmy Merrill and Joseph Brodsky: they did come to me as powerful shocks. Jimmy's death was itself shrouded by the fact that it took place miles away from all but one person who knew him, out in the southwest where we were led to believe he had gone on a holiday. There were no reports until the very end that anything was amiss. Joseph's health, of course, had been a well-known problem for a long time. He'd undergone two by-pass operations and was readying himself for a third at the time he died. He was a hopelessly addicted smoker, who flatly disregarded the repeated advice of his friends and doctors to stop. He believed, as most addicted smokers do (I was one and believed the same) that he wouldn't be able to write if he quit. I remember once saying to him that if he got married, he would surely quit; to which he replied, 'That's a poor reason to get married.' I first met Jimmy in Rome in 1950; I met Joseph at Harvard when I was teaching there in 1973 and he was newly arrived in America. He had been invited by Harvard to read, and he asked me shyly, in the most touching and diffident way, if I would be willing to read the English translations of the poems he intended to read in Russian. We were friends ever after, and like Jimmy, he was a guest at our house whenever he was in any town we were living in. Both of them died prematurely. Their absence is something I continue to feel.

I'd like to ask you about another of the poems in Proust on Skates: *'Matisse: Blue Interior with Two Girls — 1947'. How did you come to write about this painting? It's not one of Matisse's better-known works, is it?*

The painting is in Iowa. Jorie Graham at one time conceived the idea of assembling an anthology of poems based on paintings at the University of Iowa Museum of Art. She kindly inquired whether I would be interested in taking part, and sent me a handsome catalogue with colour reproductions of a hundred and one works of art, most but not all of them modern. I was invited to pick any one I liked, though clearly Jorie was anxious that I not duplicate the choice of anyone else. She set me no limits, however, and when I chose the Matisse she wrote to say she was delighted, and that no one else had picked it so it was firmly mine.

I've seen the catalogue, and the painting would seem to be one of a sequence Matisse completed while still living at Villa Le Rêve in Vence. Like the others, it shows a room occupied by two young women who are seated at a table, their backs turned on an open window through which we can see a garden. On the table in front of them are an open book and a plant-filled vase. What was it about this scene that so attracted you?

Cézanne is reported to have said, 'Painting from Nature is not copying the object; it is realizing one's sensations.' I find that a very eloquent statement. I think Cézanne might not have much cared for Matisse's work, which he would probably have found too decorative, too indifferent to dimensionality. Nevertheless, if you think about Cézanne's statement objectively, it would apply to Constable, to Poussin, to Turner supremely, but also to Frederic Church and Edward Hopper. Probably there is no way simply to 'copy the object' and do no more, even by such painters as William Harnett and John Peto, with their *trompe l'oeil* skills. The Matisse, in any case, seems to me full of feeling, and the feeling, if not quite of *luxe, calme et volupté*, is at least tranquil, serene and untroubled. Of course, there is a good deal of *volupté* in some of his odalisques, if not in the 'Blue Interior'.

You have never been content merely to describe the works of art that figure in your ecphrastic poems. And in treating the garden seen through the window as a metaphor for the world of our everyday yearnings — each of its inhabitants, 'if we take but thought, is a lean gnomon, / A bone finger with its moral point: / The hour, the minute, the dissolving pleasure' — and in treating the room itself as a metaphor for the world of aesthetic contemplation — each of its occupants 'have settled here / In this blue room of thought, beyond the reach / Of the small brief sad ambitions of the flesh' — you are clearly doing a great deal more than that here.

I'm curious, though: how would you characterize the something extra? Presumably not as a making explicit of what Matisse left implicit? After all, this was the painter who wrote in his notebook: 'What I dream of is an art of balance, of purity and serenity devoid of troubling or depressing subject matter' ...

You're right: I'm not trying to amplify Matisse's view of what he is doing. Any comment on art, whether in a poem or critical analysis, becomes to some degree the 'something extra' you speak of, if only because nothing will convey exactly the quality and nature of the painting but the painting itself. Anything else is addition (or subtraction, but at least alteration, and therefore addition of a kind). Hence the perpetuation of the critical endeavour, and the eternal employment of critics.

But let me try to respond to your complex question in a different way. There's a fine, subtle and lovely poem by Hardy called 'A Light Snow-Fall After Frost' that I would like to quote a small part of.

On the flat road a man at last appears:
How much his whitening hairs
Owe to the settling snow's mute anchorage,
And how much to a life's rough pilgrimage,
One cannot certify.

The frost is on the wane,
And cobwebs hanging close outside the pane
Pose as festoons of thick white worsted there,
Of their pale presence no eye being aware
Till the rime made them plain.

There's much to admire in these lines alone, which compose slightly less than half the poem. One is struck, for example, by that dangling, unmated rhyme at the end of the first stanza, alone in a context in which all other lines are awarded rhyming mates. That isolation will be amply rewarded in the eleventh, fourteenth and fifteenth lines, which I've left unquoted. By not quoting them now, I only emphasize the suspense and state of expectation in which the ear is held, waiting for a resolution, much as a plot leads us to expect some denouement. But other features arouse our sense of drama. That 'at last' in the first line suggests that the speaker had been at the window a long time, waiting. But it appears he is not expecting a guest; he is merely looking. And very patiently, apparently. Patiently enough to have been vouchsafed a small epiphany: the revelation of the cobwebs, unnoticed earlier, now exposed as the 'festoons of thick white worsted,' a wonderful image in its homely simplicity and 'justness'. Looking long and thoughtfully may lead to discoveries. And the discoveries themselves may be difficult to decipher, as the rest of the poem is destined to make clear. But we may begin with the initial drama of a man looking out of a window, at another world, different from the warm, unchanging interior of the room in which he stands. Two worlds, one seen through the aperture of a window from the point of view of another. This is, in essence, what Matisse's painting suggests to me. And not this painting by Matisse alone. For one thing, as you have pointed out, he has done other paintings with views from windows. So has Bonnard. So have many Renaissance portraitists. It's a very fertile notion. The framed view through the window can be a happy prospect of a rich man's estate. The mirrored view, not only of a scene of sexual dalliance but of a window beyond, through which we can see the freshness of a summer's greenery in 'The Awakening Conscience' by Holman Hunt is another instance. As is an 'Annunciation' by Rogier van der Weyden. There are too many varied examples to go on itemizing. All of them present what amounts to a double-vision, a perspective upon two worlds beheld simultaneously. In the 'Blue Interior' of Matisse, the cool blue room contrasts dramatically with the intensity of the bright greenness of out-of-doors, and the prominent diagonals of the shutters help to suggest that there is heat outside, as contrasted with the comfort of the room itself. From the opposition of heat and coolness it is but a step to the double-vision of Keats's Grecian Urn, where the warm and appetitive life is pictured but unfelt, where life and art are juxtaposed, as they are also in Yeats's 'The Dolls' and 'Sailing To Byzantium'. I could well imagine an art critic feeling that all this commentary of mine was utterly irrelevant; that Matisse was intent on painting a tranquil and harmonious picture, and that he felt his green (outside) worked harmoniously with his blue (inside) and that nothing else was of concern to him. That's perfectly okay with me. I was busy making a poem, and took my occasion from a painting and what it suggested to me.

I remember reading Stevens's letters a few years back, and discovering, to my amazement, that 'Angel Surrounded by Paysans' had as its occa-sion a still-life by Pierre Tal Coat. Have you ever written an ecphrastic poem without giving any clue that this is what you were doing?

It is funny you should ask me that. I recently finished a villanelle based on a painting which my wife and I saw during a trip to Rochester. The paint-ing was by Winslow Homer, and my poem seemed faithful enough – I relied on careful study of the work while in the gallery, and on careful scrutiny of a reliable colour reproduction which I have at home – to go by the title, 'A Winslow Homer'. Unfortunately, I had not looked at the paint-ing's title (titles of paintings rarely say anything significant, and I often ignore them); when I did look, I discovered that it made hash of my poem, for 'The Artist's Studio in an Afternoon Fog' is at something of a remove from the 'shadowy dwelling, barely seen', which in my poem 'seems cloaked in the forbidding glare / Of moonlight'. So, I had to cast around for a title that had no bearing on the Homer painting, and settled on 'Nocturne: A Recurring Dream'. No-one who hadn't heard this story could guess at the connection.

Indeed.

I suppose this might be a grotesque example of what Harold Bloom was thinking about in *A Map of Misreading.*

Do you ever think about writing your memoirs?

No, I don't, and for a number of reasons. First of all, my memory is far from perfect, which means both that I have forgotten a lot (in some re-gards, mercifully) and that memory plays tricks of its own, and I'm aware of how playful and deceitful mine has been. Secondly, the truth of the matter is that mine has been a comparatively uneventful life. Anthony Burgess has written a very lively autobiography, and he had plenty of material to work with. My life would seem very pale by comparison. Finally, there are a number of things I simply don't want to say, not least because they would cause pain to others. And those seem to me enough reasons.

Can you tell us what you are working on at the moment, and what else you have planned?

The *Florilegium* will serve as the first part of a projected new book of poems. I've not thought much beyond that point. But in a quiet way I would like to add that I'm pleased to find that at the age of seventy-five I'm able, like Herbert, to say, 'And now in age I bud again, / After so many deaths I live and write ...'

Writing is still a source of great pleasure, obviously ...

One of the great satisfactions of writing poetry consists in the absolute and indispensable conviction, while one is writing, that one is working at one's very best. To think otherwise is deeply discouraging, and virtually intolerable. But to feel one is working at one's best is to call into question the fact that one felt this way about each and every poem one had written in the past, not all of them still regarded with pride or satisfaction, and some of them, alas, now disappointing if not humiliating. This does not bear much dwelling upon.

Anthony Hecht, thank you very much.

□

An Orphic Calling

for Mihaly Csikszentmihalyi

The stream's *courante* runs on, a *force majeure,*
A Major rippling of the pure mind of Bach,
Tumult of muscled currents, formed in far
Reaches of edelweiss, cloud and alpenstock,

Now folding into each other, flexing, swirled
In cables of perdurable muscle-tones,
Hurrying through this densely noted world,
Small chambers, studio mikes, Concorde head-phones,

And from deep turbulent rapids, roiled and spun,
They rise in watery cycles to those proud
And purifying heights where they'd begun
On Jungfrau cliffs of edelweiss and cloud,

Piled cumuli, that *fons et origo*
('Too lofty and original to rage')
Of the mind's limpid unimpeded flow
Where freedom and necessity converge

And meet in a fresh curriculum of love
(Minor in grief, major in happiness)
As interlocking melodies contrive
Small trysts and liaisons, briefly digress

But only to return to Interlaken
Altitudes of clear trebles, crystal basses,
Fine reconciliations and unbroken
Threadings of fern-edged flutes down tumbling races.

An Orphic calling it is, one that invites
Responsories, a summons to lute-led
Nature, as morning's cinnabar east ignites
And the instinctive sunflower turns its head.

Anthony Hecht

With his mother, grandmother and great-grandmother, 1923

With his mother, 1925

With his father, 1925

1925

1927 or 1928

With his younger brother Roger, crossing the Atlantic, 1928

Roger Hecht, late 1930s

1943

3rd Platoon, C Company, 386th Infantry Regiment, 97th Division, US Army,
Fort Leonard Wood, Missouri, 1944 (AH third from left standing)

1946 or 1947

Ischia, 1949

Ischia, 1954

En route to Europe, circa 1950

Villa D'Este, Tivoli, 1955

Mid-1960s
photograph by Rollie McKenna ©

Mid-1960s
photograph by Rollie McKenna ©

With W.H. Auden, backstage at the 92nd Street Poetry Center in New York City, 1967
courtesy of the photographer, Jill Krementz ©

circa 1970

1970s

1970s

With his son Evan, 1975

Teaching at the University of Rochester, 1977
courtesy of the Department of Rare Books and Special Collections, University of Rochester Library ©

At the Library of Congress, Washington D.C., 1981
photograph by William Stafford ©

With Howard Moss and May Swenson, Guggenhem Museum, New York, 1985
courtesy of the photographer, Dorothy Alexander ©

With Howard Nemerov, Library of Congress, late 1980s
courtesy of the Library of Congress ©

With James Merrill (centre) and Mark Strand, Library of Congress, 1990
courtesy of the Library of Congress ©

With his wife Helen, Sewanee Writers' Conference, Tennessee, 1992
courtesy of the photographer, James R. Peters ©

American Academy of Arts & Letters, Literary Awards Committee, 1998
Standing: William Weaver, AH; Sitting: Charles Simic, Albert Murray, Robert Stone
courtesy of the photographer, Benjamin Dimmitt ©

Helen Hecht, attending a dinner at the American Academy of Arts & Letters, 1998
courtesy of the photographer, Dorothy Alexander ©

Evan Hecht and his father, at his father's 75th birthday party, 1998
courtesy of the photographer, Dorothy Alexander ©

At his 75th birthday party, 1998
courtesy of the photographer, Dorothy Alexander ©

Washington D.C., 2001
courtesy of the photographer, Philip Hoy ©

Bibliography

While everything has been done to ensure the completeness and accuracy of this bibliography, the editors can be sure that their efforts have not been entirely successful. They would therefore be pleased to hear from anyone who can identify omissions or errors, which it would be their hope to repair in future editions.

PRIMARY WORKS

POETRY

BOOKS

A Summoning of Stones, Macmillan, New York, 1954.
The Seven Deadly Sins, with wood engravings by Leonard Baskin, The Gehenna Press, Northampton, Massachusetts, 1958.
Struwwelpeter, with illustrations by Leonard Baskin, The Gehenna Press, Northampton, Massachusetts, 1958.
A Bestiary, with twenty illustrations by Aubrey Schwartz, Kanthos Press, Los Angeles, California, 1962.
Aesopic, twenty-four couplets accompanying Thomas Bewick's wood engravings for selected fables, with an afterword on the blocks by Philip Hofer, The Gehenna Press, Northampton, Massachusetts, 1967.
The Hard Hours, Atheneum, New York, 1967; O.U.P., Oxford, 1967.
Millions of Strange Shadows, Atheneum, New York, 1977; O.U.P., Oxford, 1977.
The Venetian Vespers, with six illustrations by Dimitri Hadzi, David R. Godine, Boston, 1979.
The Venetian Vespers (and other poems), Atheneum, New York, 1979; O.U.P., Oxford, 1980.
A Love for Four Voices: Homage to Franz Joseph Haydn, Mandeville Press, Hitchin, Hertfordshire, 1983.
The Book of Yolek, Emory University, Atlanta, Georgia, 1990.
Collected Earlier Poems, Knopf, New York, 1990; O.U.P., Oxford, 1991.
The Transparent Man, Knopf, New York, 1990; O.U.P., Oxford, 1991.
The Presumptions of Death, The Gehenna Press, Rockport, Maine, 1995.
Flight Among the Tombs, Knopf, New York, 1996; O.U.P., Oxford, 1997.
A Gehenna Florilegium, The Gehenna Press, Rockport, Maine, 1998.
The Darkness and the Light, Knopf, New York, 2001.

BROADSIDES

From 'A Little Cemetery', International Poetry Forum, Pittsburgh, Pennsylvania, 1976.
'Horace I:22, or words to that effect', *Northern Lights: Broadside Poems*, Palaemon Press, Winston, Salem, North Carolina, 1983.
'Humoresque', privately printed for A.H., 1983.

'Curriculum Vitae', Palaeman Press, Winston, Salem, North Carolina, 1984; Knopf, New York, 1990.
'Death Sauntering About', Friends of the Amherst College Library, Amherst, Massachusetts, 1994.
'Once More, With Feeling', Aralia Press, 1998.

UNCOLLECTED

'A Little Cemetery', Counter / Measures 1, 1972, 15; one of the poems in this sequence is reprinted in Tygers of Wrath, edited by X.J. Kennedy, The University of Georgia Press, Athens, Georgia, 1981, 9.
'On Translation – for Robert Fitzgerald', Poetry, 141:1, 1982, 11.
'Indolence', The New Yorker, 74:13, May 25 ,1998, 76.
'The Wise', The New Yorker, 74:13, May 25, 1998, 90.
'Long-Distance Vision', The Hudson Review, 51:1, Spring 1998, 148.
'A Certain Slant', The Sewanee Review, Fall 1998.
'Witness', Poetry Review, 88, 1998, 26.
'Look Deep', The Yale Review, 86:3, 1998, 29-30.
'A Fall', The Yale Review, 86:3, 1998, 31-32
'Illumination', The New Yorker, December 28, 1998 – January 4, 1999.
'The Hanging Gardens at Tyburn', Stand, new series, 1:1, March 1999, 91.

TRANSLATIONS

BOOKS

Seven Against Thebes [Aeschylus], with Helen Bacon, O.U.P., New York, 1973; O.U.P., Oxford, 1974.
Voltaire's Poème sur le désastre de Lisbonne / Poem upon the Lisbon Disaster, with six wood engravings by Lynd Ward and an introduction by Arthur Wilson, Penmaen Press, 1977.
A Part of Speech [Joseph Brodsky], with George Kline, Howard Moss, Alan Myers, David Rigsbee, Barry Rubin, Daniel Weissbort and Richard Wilbur, Farrar, Strauss and Giroux, New York, 1980; O.U.P., Oxford, 1980; reissued, with foreword by A.H. 1997.

UNCOLLECTED

'Le Jet d'eau' (Baudelaire), The Paris Review, 148, Fall 1998.
'The Plastic and the Poetic Form' (Goethe), The Formalist, 9:1, 1998.
'Dawn's Twilight' (Baudelaire), The Formalist, 9:1, 1998.
'The Bequest' (Vaillant), The Formalist, 9:2, 1998.
'Once More, With Feeling', (Charles d'Orléans), The Formalist, 9:2, 1998.
'Taking Charge' (Charles d'Orléans), The Formalist, 9:2, 1998.

EDITIONS

Jiggery-Pokery: A Compendium of Double Dactyls, with John Hollander, illustrations by
Milton Glaser, Atheneum, New York, 1967; reissued 1984.
The Essential Herbert, Ecco Press, New York, The Essential Poets Series, Vol. 5, 1987.

MUSICAL SETTINGS

Foss, Lukas, *Parable of Death / Ein Märchen Vom Tod,* for narrator, chorus, tenor solo and
orchestra, based on a story and poems by Rainer Maria Rilke, English translation
by A.H., score published by C. Fischer, New York, 1953.
Leo Smit, *A Serenata for Four Voices and Ten Instruments,* for unaccompanied chorus,
words by A.H. (entitled 'A Choir of Starlings'), score published by C. Fischer,
New York, 1977.
Beaser, Robert, *The Seven Deadly Sins,* for tenor or baritone and piano, a setting of A.H.'s
'Seven Deadly Sins', score published by Helicon, New York, 1979; featured on
a CD of Beaser's works, Argo (440-337-2), 1994.

THEATRICAL PERFORMANCES

'A Love for Four Voices', Greenwich Village Theatre, a single performance, directed by
Troy Holler, February 14, 1996.

PROSE

BOOKS

Obbligati: Essays in Criticism, Atheneum, New York, 1986.
The Hidden Law: The Poetry of W.H. Auden, Harvard University Press, Cambridge, Mas-
sachusetts, and London, 1993.
On The Laws of the Poetic Art: The Andrew Mellon Lectures in the Fine Arts, Princeton
University Press, Princeton, New Jersey, 1995.

FORTHCOMING

Melodies Unheard, Johns Hopkins University Press, Baltimore, Maryland, Date To Be An-
nounced.

FOREWORDS, INTRODUCTIONS, PREFACES

de la Mare, Walter, *Songs of Childhood,* Garland Publishing Co., New York and London,

1976.

Aaron, Jonathan, *Second Sight*, Harper & Row, New York, 1982.

The Morrow Anthology of Younger American Poets, edited by Dave Smith and David Bottoms, Wiliam Morrow & Co., New York, 1985.

Donnelly, Susan, *Eve Names the Animals*, Northeastern University Press, Boston, Massachusetts, 1985.

Plutzik, Hyam, *The Collected Poems*, BOA Editions, Brockport, New York, 1987.

Shakespeare, William, *The Sonnets*, edited by G. Blakemore Evans, C.U.P., Cambridge,1996.

Brodsky, Joseph, *A Part of Speech*, O.U.P., New York and Oxford, 1997.

Fairchild, B.H., *The Art of the Lathe*, Alice James Books, 1998.

Discussions, Essays, Reviews

Aiken, Conrad, *A Letter from Li Po & Other Poems*, The Hudson Review, 9:3, Autumn 1956, 447-48.

Bell, Charles, *Delta Return*, The Hudson Review, 9:3, Autumn 1956, 456.

Bishop, Elizabeth, *North & South* and *A Cold Spring*, The Hudson Review, 9:3, Autumn 1956, 456.

Ciardi, John, *As If* , The Hudson Review, Autumn 1956, 449-50.

Cole, Thomas, *A World of Saints*, The Hudson Review, 9:3, Autumn 1956, 452-53.

Hoskins, Katherine, *Villa Narcisse*, The Hudson Review, 9:3, Autumn 1956, 450-51.

Mickiewicz, Adam, *Selected Poems*, The Hudson Review 9:3, Autumn 1956, 446-47.

Miles, Josephine, *Prefabrications*, The Hudson Review 9:3, Autumn 1956, 451.

Muir, Edwin, *One Foot in Eden*, The Hudson Review 9:3, Autumn 1956, 448-49.

Palmer, Winthrop, *Fables and Ceremonies* , The Hudson Review, 9:3, Autumn 1956, 454.

Watson, Katherine, *The Source and Other Poems*, The Hudson Review, 9:3, Autumn 1956.

Whittemore, Reed, *An American Takes a Walk*, The Hudson Review, 9:3, Autumn 1956, 452.

Wilbur, Richard, *Things of This World*, The Hudson Review, 9:3, Autumn 1956, 454-55.

Williams, Tennessee, *In the Winter of Cities*, The Hudson Review, 9:3, Autumn 1956, 456-57.

Williams, William Carlos, *Journey to Love*, The Hudson Review, 9:3, Autumn 1956, 444-46.

Lattimore, Richmond, *Poems*, The Hudson Review, 10:4, Winter 1957-58, 606-13.

Siegel, Eli, *Hot Afternoons Have Been in Montana*, The Hudson Review, 10:4, Winter 1957-58, 606-13.

Stevens, Wallace, *Opus Posthumous*, The Hudson Review, 10:4, Winter 1957-58, 606-13.

Warren, Robert Penn, *Promises: Poems 1954-1956*, The Hudson Review, 10:4, Winter 1957-58, 606-13.

Hall, Donald, *The Dark Houses*, The Hudson Review, 11:4, Winter 1958-59, 635-36.

Heath-Stubbs, John, *The Triumph of the Muse*, The Hudson Review, 11:4, Winter 1958-59, 634-35.

MacNeice, Louis, *Visitations*, The Hudson Review, 11:4, Winter 1958-59, 631-34.

Swenson, May, *A Cage of Spines*, The Hudson Review, 11:4, Winter 1958-59, 635-36.

Wagoner, David, *A Place to Stand*, The Hudson Review, 11:4, Winter 1958-59, 635-36.

'A Few Green Leaves' [an essay in celebration of Allen Tate's sixtieth birthday], *The Sewanee Review*, 67:4, Autumn 1959, 568-571.

Huff, Robert, *Colonel Johnson's Ride*, The Hudson Review, 12:4, Winter 1959-60, 593-603.

Kerouac, Jack, *Mexico City Blues, The Hudson Review*, 12:4, Winter 1959-60, 593-603.
Moore, Marianne, *O to be a Dragon, The Hudson Review*, 12:4, Winter 1959-60, 593-603.
Nabokov, Vladimir, *Poems, The Hudson Review*, 12:4, Winter 1959-60, 593-603.
Schwartz, Delmore, *Summer Knowledge, The Hudson Review*, 12:4, Winter 1959-60, 593-603.
Simpson, Louis, *A Dream of Governors, The Hudson Review*, 12:4, Winter 1959-60, 593-603.
Wright, James, *Saint Judas, The Hudson Review*, 12:4, Winter 1959-60, 593-603; a shortened version was reprinted in *James Wright: The Heart of the Light*, edited by Peter Stitt and Frank Graziano, The University of Michigan Press, 1990.
Creekmore, Hubert, editor, *Lyrics of the Middle Ages, The Hudson Review*, 13:1, Spring 1960, 131-38.
Rilke, Rainer Maria, *The Lay of the Love and Death of Cornet Christopher Rilke*, translated by Mary Dows Herter Norton, *The Hudson Review*, 13:1, Spring 1960, 131-38.
Rothenberg, Jerome, *New Young German Poets, The Hudson Review*, 13:1, Spring 1960, 131-38.
'Shades of Keats and Marvell', *The Hudson Review*, 15, Spring 1962, 50-71.
'Note on "The Vow"', in *Poet's Choice*, edited by Paul Engle and Joseph Langland, Dell Publishing, New York, 1962, 200-201.
'On The Methods and Ambitions of Poetry', *The Hudson Review*, 18, Winter 1965-66, 489-505.
'Double Dactyl', *Esquire*, 65, June 1966, 109+.
Finkel, Donald, *A Joyful Noise, The Hudson Review*, 19:1, Summer 1966, 330-38.
Grass, Günter, *Selected Poems, The Hudson Review*, 19:2, Summer 1966, 330-38.
Haines, John, *Winter News, The Hudson Review*, 19:2, Summer 1966, 330-38.
Merrill, James, *Nights and Days, The Hudson Review*, 19:2, Summer 1966, 330-38.
Nemerov, Howard, *Poets on Poetry, The Hudson Review*, 19:2, Summer 1966, 330-38.
Silkin, Jon, *Poems, The Hudson Review*, 19:2, Summer 1966, 330-38.
Wain, John, *Wildtrack, The Hudson Review*, 19:2, Summer 1966, 330-38.
'I Hear America Singing Slightly Off-Key', *Esquire*, 66, September 1966, 164-67.
Auden, W.H., *Selected Shorter Poems 1927-1957, The Hudson Review*, 21:1, Spring 1968, 207-17.
Dugan, Alan, *Poems 3, The Hudson Review*, 21:1, Spring 1968, 207-17.
Hughes, Ted, *Wodwo, The Hudson Review*, 21:1, Spring 1968, 207-17.
Moore, Marianne, *The Collected Poems of Marianne Moore, The Hudson Review*, 21:1, Spring 1968, 207-17.
Nemerov, Howard, *The Blue Swallows, The Hudson Review*, 21:1, Spring 1968, 207-17.
Sissman, L.E., *Dying: An Introduction, The Hudson Review*, 21:1, Spring 1968, 207-17.
'Discovering Auden', *Harvard Advocate*, 108, 1975, 48-50.
'The Belle of Amherst', *TV Guide*, December 18, 1976.
Wilbur, Richard, *The Mind Reader, The Times Literary Supplement*, May 20, 1977, 602.
Bishop, Elizabeth, *Geography III, The Times Literary Supplement*, August 26, 1977.
'The Riddles of Emily Dickinson', *New England Review*, 1, Autumn 1978, 1-24; reprinted in *Emily Dickinson: A Collection of Critical Essays*, edited by Judith Farr, Prentice Hall, Englewood Cliffs, New Jersey, 1996.
'On W.H. Auden's "In Praise of Limestone"', *New England Review*, 2, 1979, 65-84.
'John Crowe Ransom', *American Scholar*, 49:3, Summer 1980, 379-83.
'Masters of Unpleasantness: The Making of a Writer', *New York Times Book Review*, 87:6, February 7, 1982, 3+.

'My Most Obnoxious Writer', *New York Times Book Review*, 87:35, August 29, 1982, 7+.

'Elbert Weinburg', *Arts Magazine*, 57:4, November 1982, 4.

'Books That Gave Me Pleasure', *New York Times Book Review*, 87, December 5, 1982, 9+.

'Matthew Arnold', *New York Times Book Review*, 1982.

Hamilton, Ian, *Robert Lowell: A Biography*, Grand Street, 2, Spring 1983, 32-48.

'Symposium of Poets on T.S. Eliot: Permanent Surprise' [an essay on the opening lines of *The Waste Land*], *The Southern Review*, 21:4, 1985, 1146-1148.

'The Pathetic Fallacy', *The Yale Review*, 74:4, Summer 1985, 481-99.

Ackroyd, Peter, *T.S. Eliot: A Biography*, The Washington Post, Book World, 16, November 23, 1986, 1-14.

Wilbur, Richard, *New and Collected Poems*, The New Republic, 198:20, May 16, 1988, 23-32.

Giroux, Robert, editor, *Collected Prose: Robert Lowell*, The New York Review of Books 35:3, March 3, 1988, 11-17.

Sullivan, Walter, *Allen Tate: A Recollection*, The Washington Times, January 23, 1989, 7-10.

Ellmann, Richard, *a long the riverrun: Selected Essays*, The Washington Post, Book World, March 26, 1989, 10.

Rowse, A.L., *The Poet Auden: A Personal Memoir*, The New York Review of Books, 36:20, December 21, 1989, 56-59.

'The First Eighteen Lines of "The Waste Land"', *The Yale Review*, 78:2, The T.S. Eliot Memorial Issue, September 1989, 202-209.

Essay on the *Epistle to the Galatians*, in *Incarnation: Contemporary Writers on the New Testament*, edited by Alfred Corn, Viking Press, New York, 1990.

'O.B. Hardison (1928-1990) – In Memoriam', *The Sewanee Review*, 99:1, 1991, 164-165.

'Comments on the Practice of Alluding', *University of Toronto Quarterly*, 61:3, Spring 1992, 381-385.

'From Etymology to Paronomasia' [reply to Eleanor Cook], *Connotation*, Münster, Germany, 2:2, 201-04, 1992.

'A Hundred Years After: Twelve Writers Reflect on Tennyson's Achievement and Influence', *The Times Literary Supplement*, 4670, 1992, 8-9.

'Arrowsmith at Colonus', *Arion*, 2:2-3, 1993, 231-234.

'John Crowe Ransom', *The Wilson Quarterly*, 18, Spring 1994.

'Katherine Hoskins', *The Wilson Quarterly*, 18, Summer 1994.

'As He Laid Down His Pen – Comment', *New York Times Book Review*, January 1994, 35.

'Ben Jonson', *The Wilson Quarterly*, 19, Spring 1995, 97-98.

'George Starbuck', *The Wilson Quarterly*, 19, Summer 1995.

'L.E. Sissman', *The Wilson Quarterly*, 19, Winter 1995, 120-122.

'History as Drama', *American Heritage*, 46:4, July-August, 1995, 8.

'Memorial Tribute to James Merrill', *Poetry*, 166:6, 1995, 339.

'The Poetic Heritage – Reply', *New York Times Book Review*, January 1996, 5.

Davenport-Hines, Richard, *Auden*, The Yale Review, 84:3, July 1996.

'Carl Dennis', *The Wilson Quarterly*, 20, Summer 1996, 90-91.

'Joseph Brodsky', *The Wilson Quarterly*, 20, Winter 1996, 104-106.

'Gaze not on Swans', in *Touchstones: American Poets on a Favorite Poem*, edited by Robert Pack and Jay Parini, University Press of New England, 1996.

'Meditation', in *Ecstatic Occasions, Expedient Forms: 85 Leading Contemporary Poets Select and Comment on Their Poems*, edited by David Lehman, The University of

Michigan Press, Ann Arbor, Michigan, 1996.
'Joseph Brodsky, 1940-1996: A Tribute', *Poetry Review*, 86:1, 35-36, 1996.
'Walter de la Mare', *The Wilson Quarterly*, 21, Summer 1997, 108-109.
'May Swenson', *The Wilson Quarterly*, 21, Winter 1997, 105-106.
'The Sonnet: Ruminations on Form, Sex, and History', *The Antioch Review*, Spring 1997.
'Eugenio Montale', *The Wilson Quarterly*, 22, Summer 1998, 111-112.
'Horace', *The Wilson Quarterly*, 22, Winter 1998, 110-114.
'Missing the Boat', in *Night Errands: How Poets Use Dreams*, edited by Roderick Townley, University of Pittsburgh Press, 1998.
'On Rhyme', *The Yale Review*, 87:2, April 1999.

AUTOBIOGRAPHICAL NOTES

The Poetry Book Society Bulletin, 55, December 1967.
The Poetry Book Society Bulletin, 104, Spring 1980.

RECORDINGS

AUDIOTAPES

Reading by A.H., Northampton, Massachusetts, 1958.
Reading by A.H. of 'The Vow', 'A Hill', 'A Letter', Spoken Arts SA1054, 1969.
Reading by A.H. and Barbara Howes, The Library of Congress, Washington D.C., Coolidge Auditorium, October 19, 1970.
Reading by A.H., Breadloaf School of English, Vermont, 1973.
Reading by A.H., Worcester Poetry Festival, Worcester Public Library, Massachusetts, May 1, 1973.
Reading by A.H., The Library of Congress, Washington D.C., Coolidge Auditorium, October 4, 1982.
Reading by A.H., The Library of Congress, Washington D.C., Studio B, October 25, 1982.
Readings by Carolyn Forché and George Starbuck, introduced by A.H., The Library of Congress, Washington D.C., Coolidge Auditorium, October 26, 1982.
Reading by Kamau Braithwaite, introduced by A.H., The Library of Congress, Washington D.C., Coolidge Auditorium, October 5, 1982.
Readings by Alfred Corn and Carl Dennis, introduced by A.H., The Library of Congress, Washington D.C., Coolidge Auditorium, November 8, 1982.
Archibald Macleish memorial program, with readings of his work by A.H., John C. Broderick, Samuel Hazo, Pat Hingle, William Meredith and Julia Randall, The Library of Congress, Washington D.C., Coolidge Auditorium, 1982.
An Evening of Scandinavian Poetry, with readings by Paal-Helge Haugen [et al], introduced by A.H., The Library of Congress, Washington D.C., Coolidge Auditorium, 1982.
Reading by A.H., The Library of Congress, Washington D.C., Coolidge Auditorium, 1982.
Readings by Richard Murphy and Jon Stallworthy, introduced by A.H., The Library of Congress, Washington D.C., Coolidge Auditorium, February 22, 1983.

'Oscar Wilde at Oxford: A Lecture' by Richard Ellmann, introduced by A.H., The Library of Congress, Washington D.C., Coolidge Auditorium, March 1, 1983.

Reading by Ralph Ellison from a novel in progress, introduced by A.H., The Library of Congress, Washington D.C., Coolidge Auditorium, March 28, 1983.

Readings by Alicia Ostriker and Dave Smith, introduced by A.H., The Library of Congress, Washington D.C., Coolidge Auditorium, April 11, 1983.

Lecture by Stephen Spender on poetry and political events in the 1930s, with readings of W.H. Auden, C. Day-Lewis and others, introduced by A.H., The Library of Congress, Washington D.C., Coolidge Auditorium, April 19, 1983.

'Robert Lowell', a lecture by A.H., with readings from Lowell's poetry, introduced by John C. Broderick, The Library of Congress, Washington D.C., Coolidge Auditorium, May 2, 1983.

Reading by A.H., introduced by John C. Broderick, The Library of Congress, Washington D.C., Coolidge Auditorium, October 3, 1983.

Readings by A.H. of poems by Wallace Stevens, Elizabeth Bishop, Samuel Johnson, Howard Nemerov and James Wright, with musical interludes featuring the pianist Frank Glazer, The Library of Congress, Washington D.C., Coolidge Auditorium, October 25, 1983.

Reading by Shirley Hazzard, introduced by A.H., The Library of Congress, Washington D.C., Coolidge Auditorium, December 5, 1983.

'William Carlos Williams: "The Happy Genius of the Household": A Centennial Lecture' by Reed Whittemore, introduced by A.H., The Library of Congress, Washington D.C., Coolidge Auditorium, November 1, 1983.

Academy of American Poets, 50th Anniversary Celebration, with readings by Robert Fitzgerald, Daniel Hoffman, John Hollander, Stanley Kunitz, James Merrill, Howard Nemerov, and Mona Van Duyn, introduced by A.H., The Library of Congress, Washington D.C., Coolidge Auditorium, November 14, 1983.

Readings by Sydney Lea and David St. John, The Library of Congress, Washington D.C., Coolidge Auditorium, November 29, 1983.

Readings by Amy Clampitt and Robert Pinsky, introduced by A.H., The Library of Congress, Washington D.C., Coolidge Auditorium, February 27, 1984.

'W.B. Yeats's Second Puberty: A Lecture' by Richard Ellmann, introduced by A.H., The Library of Congress, Washington D.C., Coolidge Auditorium, April 2, 1984.

Reading by Bernard Malamud of two short stories, introduced by A.H., The Library of Congress, Washington D.C., Studio B, April 24, 1984.

Reading by Joseph Brodsky of six of his poems, preceded by A.H. reading their English translations, The Library of Congress, Washington D.C., Coolidge Auditorium, April 16, 1984.

'The Social Authority of the Writer', a lecture by Northrop Frye, introduced by A.H., The Library of Congress, Washington D.C., Coolidge Auditorium, April 24, 1984.

Readings by A.H. and others, celebrating the 60th anniversary of the Academy of American Poetry, The Library of Congress, Washington D.C., Coolidge Auditorium,1984.

Reading by A.H., introduced by Howard Moss, The Library of Congress, Washington D.C., Coolidge Auditorium, October 28, 1985.

Reading by A.H., *The Spoken Arts Treasury of 100 Modern American Poets Reading Their Poetry*, Spoken Arts, New Rochelle, NY, 1985.

Reading by A.H., New York Poetry Center, January 19, 1987.

Readings by A.H. and others, celebrating the 50th anniversary of the Consultancy in Poetry, The Library of Congress, Washington D.C., Coolidge Auditorium, 1988.

Readings by A.H. and Joseph Brodsky, New York Poetry Center, October 17, 1988.
Reading by A.H. of other writers' light verse, The Library of Congress, Washington D.C., Coolidge Auditorium, December 13, 1988.
'New Letters on the Air: Anthony Hecht', a radio programme hosted by Rebekah Presson and featuring A.H. in interview with Robert Aubry Davis, broadcast March 1988, University of Missouri, Kansas City, Missouri, 1988.
Reading by A.H., introduced by J.D. McClatchy, The Academy of American Poets, Pierpoint Morgan Library, January 24, 1991.
Readings by A.H. and Joseph Brodsky, introduced by J.D. McClatchy, New York Poetry Center, December 22, 1991.
Readings by A.H. of poems by Wyatt, Shakespeare, Donne, Marvell and Hopkins, *The Classic Hundred Poems*, Columbia University Press, Highbridge Co., 1998.
Craft Lecture by A.H., Sewanee Writers' Conference, Sewanee, Tennessee, July 22, 1992.
Reading by A.H., Sewanee Writers' Conference, Sewanee, Tennessee, August 1, 1992.
Reading by A.H., Sewanee Writers' Conference, Sewanee, Tennessee, July 22, 1993.
Craft Lecture by A.H., Sewanee Writers' Conference, Sewanee, Tennessee, July 29, 1994.
Reading by A.H., Sewanee Writers' Conference, Sewanee, Tennessee, July 30, 1994.
Reading by A.H., Sewanee Writers' Conference, Sewanee, Tennessee, July 25, 1995.
Craft Lecture by A.H., Sewanee Writers' Conference, Sewanee, Tennessee, July 23, 1996.
Reading by A.H., Sewanee Writers' Conference, Sewanee, Tennessee, July 26, 1996.
Reading by A.H., Sewanee Writers' Conference, Sewanee, Tennessee, July 22, 1997.

FILMS AND VIDEOTAPES

Emily Dickinson, a film produced by the New York Center for Visual History, with appearances by A.H., 1 x 57 minute film reel / 1 x 57 minute video cassette, issued by Intellimation, Santa Barbara, California, 1987.
Robert Lowell, a film produced by the New York Center for Visual History, with appearances by A.H., Frank Bidart, and Derek Walcott, 1 x 57 minute film reel from Intellimation, Santa Barbara, California, 1987 / 1 x 57 minute video cassette, issued by Mystic Fire Video, New York, 1995.
Adam's Task, a reading of animal poems by A.H., Rachel Hadas, Vicki Hearne, John Hollander and Richard Howard, held at The New School for Social Research, New York, on April 7 1995, under the auspices of The Academy of American Poets, New York, 1 x 88 minute video cassette issued by Betelgeuse Productions, New York, 1985.

INTERVIEWS AND QUESTIONNAIRES

Gerber, Philip L., Gemmett, Robert J., 'An Interview with Anthony Hecht', *Mediterranean Review*, 1:3, 1971, 3-9.
Smith, Wendy, 'An Interview with Anthony and Helen Hecht', *Publisher's Weekly*, 230: 70-71, July 18, 1986, 70+.
McClatchy, J.D., 'The Art of Poetry XXXX: Anthony Hecht', *The Paris Review*, 108, Fall 1988, 160-205.
Davis, Robert A., 'New Letters on the Air: Anthony Hecht', a radio programme hosted by Rebekah Presson and featuring A.H. in interview, broadcast March 1988 (see

entry under audiotapes).

Baer, William, *The Formalist*, 6:2, July, 1995.

Hammer, Langdon, 'Efforts of Attention: An Interview with Anthony Hecht', *The Sewanee Review*, Winter 1996, 94-107.

Hoy, Philip, 'Anthony Hecht in Interview with Philip Hoy' (extracts from an earlier version of the interview featured in this book), *Stand*, New Series, 1:1, March 1999, 92-98.

Hoy, Philip, *Anthony Hecht in Conversation with Philip Hoy*, Between The Lines, London, 1999.

Hutner, Gordon, 'The Situation of American Writing 1999', *American Literary History*, 11:2, Summer, 1999, 276-281.

SECONDARY WORKS

Books

German, Norman, *Anthony Hecht*, American University Studies on American Literature, Series XXIV, Vol. 7, Peter Lang, New York, Bern, Frankfurt am Main, Paris, 1989, 230 pp.

Lea, Sydney, editor, *The Burdens of Formality: Essays on the Poetry of Anthony Hecht*, with contributions from Brad Leithauser, Ashley Brown, Norman Williams, Daniel Hoffman, Joseph Brodsky, Edward Hirsch, Peter Sacks, Alicia Ostriker, Linda Orr, John Frederick Nims, William Matthews, Kenneth Gross and J.D. McClatchy, University of Georgia Press, Athens, Georgia and London, 1989.

ESSAYS, ARTICLES, ENTRIES

Plath, Sylvia, 'Poets on Campus', *Mademoiselle*, 37, August 1953, 290.

Fraser, G.S., 'Some Younger American Poets', *Commentary*, 23, May 1957, 462.

Joost, Nicholas, 'Hecht's "Ostia Antica"', *The Explicator*, 20:2, September 1961, item 14.

Jennings, Elizabeth, *Every Changing Shape: Mystical Experience and the Making of Poems*, [discussion of A.H.'s 'Ostia Antica' in Chapter 2, 'Images in Abeyance: Aspects of Augustine'], André Deutsch, London, 1961; reissued by Carcanet, Manchester, 1996.

Hemphill, George, 'Anthony Hecht's Nunnery of Art', *Perspective*, 12:4, 1962, 163-171.

Hoffman, Daniel, 'Poetry of Anguish', *Reporter*, 38, February 22, 1968, 52-54.

Miller, Stephen, 'A Poem by Anthony Hecht', *Spirit* 39:1, 1972, 8-11.

Brown, Ashley, 'The Poetry of Anthony Hecht', *Ploughshares*, 4:3, 1978, 9-24; reprinted in *Modern Critical Views: Contemporary Poets*, edited and with an introduction by Harold Bloom, Chelsea House Publishers, New York and Philadelphia, 1986, 113-26, reprinted in *The Burdens of Formality*, edited by Sydney Lea, The University of Georgia Press, Athens, Georgia and London, 1989.

Hoffman, Daniel, 'Poetry: Dissidents from Schools', *Harvard Guide to Contemporary American Writing*, edited by Daniel Hoffman, Harvard University Press, Cambridge, Massachusetts, 1979, 581-586.

Atlas, James, 'New Voices in American Poetry', *New York Times Magazine,* 129, February 3, 1980, 1-6.

Brown, Ashley, 'Anthony Hecht', in the *Dictionary of Literary Biography: American Poets Since World War II,* Vol. 5, Part 1, edited by Donald J. Greiner, Book Tower, Detroit, 1980, 318-324.

Howard, Richard, 'What Do We Know of Lasting Since the Fall?' *Alone With America: Essays on the Art of Poetry in the United States Since 1950,* (enlarged edition), Atheneum, New York, 1980, 195-208.

Halpern, D., 'The Pursuit of Suffering', *Antaeus,* 40:4, 1981, 427-441.

Jacobsen, Eric, '"Look Here upon This Picture and on This"': Reflections on Some Modern Picture Poems' [includes discussion of A.H.'s 'Dichtung und Wahrheit' and 'Auguries of Innocence'], *Papers from the First Nordic Conference for English Studies,* edited by Stig Johansson and Bjorn Tysdahl, Institute of English Studies, University of Oslo, 1981.

Morris, Herbert, 'After the Reading', *New England Review and Breadloaf Quarterly,* 5:1-2, Autumn-Winter 1982, 81-85.

George, E., 'Translating Poetry – Notes on a Solitary Craft', *The Kenyon Review,* 4:2, 1982, 33-54.

'Anthony Hecht', *Contemporary Authors,* New Revision Series, Vol. 6, Book Tower, Detroit, Michigan, 1982, 221-222.

Walters, Colin, 'Anthony Hecht: Iambic Rhythm and Dignity', *Washington Times,* 1982.

Nelson, Dale, 'Bollingen Back at LC', *Wilson Library Bulletin,* 57, April 1983, 684-85.

Jerome, Judson, 'Page Turners', *Writer's Digest,* 64, August 1984, 10.

Hallberg, Robert von, *American Poetry and Culture, 1945-1980,* Harvard University Press, Cambridge, Massachusetts and London, 1985.

Steele, Peter, *Expatriates: Reflections on Modern Poetry,* Melbourne University Press, 1985.

Leithauser, Brad, 'Poet for a Dark Age', *The New York Review of Books,* 33:2, February 13, 1986, 11-12, 14.

Scupham, Peter, 'Grisaille and Millefleurs', *Poetry Review* (London), 76:3, October 1986, 9-12.

O'Brien, Timothy D., 'Hecht's "The Dover Bitch"', *Explicator,* 44:2, Winter 1986, 52-54.

Gerhard, Joseph, 'The Dover Bitch: Victorian Duck or Modernist Duck / Rabbit?', *Victorian Newsletter,* 73, Spring 1988, 8-10.

Whedon, Tony, 'Three Mannerists', *The American Poetry Review,* 17:3, May-June 1988, 41-47.

German, Norman, 'Anthony Hecht: Contemporary Transcendentalist', *Ball Street University Forum,* 30:3, Summer 1989, 46-52.

Cervo, Nathan, 'The Dover Glitch: Soul à la Sole', *Victorian Newsletter,* 76, Fall 1989, 31-33.

Corn, Alfred, 'Contemporary Poetry's Mother Tongues', *The Great Ideas Today, Encyclopaedia Britannica,* VIII, 1995, 471.

McClatchy, J.D., 'Anatomies of Melancholy', in his *White Paper: On Contemporary American Poetry,* Columbia University Press, 1989; reprinted in *The Burdens of Formality,* edited by Sydney Lea, The University of Georgia Press, Athens, GA and London, 1989.

Spiegelman, Willard, 'The Moral Imperative in Anthony Hecht, Allen Ginsberg, and Robert Pinsky', in his *The Didactic Muse: Scenes of Instruction in Contemporary American Poetry,* Princeton University Press, Princeton, New Jersey,1989.

Prunty, Wyatt, 'Fallen From the Symboled World': Precedents for the New Formalism, O.U.P., Oxford, 1990.

Corn, Alfred, 'How to Enjoy Reading Poetry Again', Poetry, 157:1, 1990, 33-50.

Taylor, Henry, 'Forms of Conviction', The Southern Review, 27:1, Winter 1991, 235-42.

Strand, Mark, 'Views of the Mysterious Hill: The Appearances of Parnassus in American Poetry', Gettysburg Review, 4:4, 1991, 669-679.

Taylor, Henry, Compulsory Figures: Essays on Recent American Poets, Louisiana State University Press, 1992.

Hollander, John, 'Anthony Hecht, "At the Frick" / Giovanni Bellini', in his The Gazer's Spirit, The University of Chicago Press, Chicago and London, 1995.

Casey, Ellen Miller, 'Hecht's "More Light! More Light!"', Explicator, 54:2, Winter 1996, 113-15.

Maxwell, Glyn, 'Anthony Hecht', The Oxford Companion to 20th-Century Poetry, edited by Ian Hamilton, O.U.P., Oxford, New York, 1996, 223-224.

Miola, Robert, 'Anthony Hecht', Contemporary Poets, 6th edition, edited by Thomas Riggs, St. James Press, Chicago and London, 1996, 463-465.

Lindsay, Geoffrey, '"Laws that stand for other laws": Anthony Hecht's Dramatic Strategy', Essays in Literature, 21:2, 1994, 285-300.

REVIEWS

A SUMMONING OF STONES (1954)

Wilbur, Richard, 'Urgency and Artifice', The New York Times Book Review, April 4, 1954, 12.

Bogan, Louise, The New Yorker, 30, June 5, 1954, 134.

Bennet, Joseph, 'Recent Verse', The Hudson Review, 7:2, Summer 1954, 306-308.

Davie, Donald, 'Book Review', Shenandoah, 8:1, Autumn 1956, 43-44.

Flint, F.W., 'Poets of the '50s', Partisan Review, 21:6, November – December 1954, 679-681.

Mizener, Arthur, 'Transformations', The Kenyon Review, 16, 1954, 479-481.

AESOPIC (1967)

Massachusetts Review, 11, Winter 1970, 97-100.

JIGGERY-POKERY (1967)

Gross, John. 'Double Dactyls and Other Wonders', New York Times Book Review, 89, January 19, 1984, 8.

THE HARD HOURS (1967)

Unsigned, 'Unamerican Editions', The Times Literary Supplement, 3:430, November 23,

1967, 1106.

Meredith, William, 'Formal Effects', *New York Times Book Review*, December 17, 1967, 24-25.

Booth, Phillip, *The Christian Science Monitor*, 9, February 1, 1968.

Thompson, John, *The New York Review of Books*, August 1, 1968, 35.

Simpson, Louis, *Harper's Magazine*, August 1968, 74.

Carruth, Hayden, 'Critic of the Month: I', *Poetry*, 112:6, September, 1968, 424.

Liebermann, Laurence, 'Recent Poetry in Review: Risks and Faiths', *The Yale Review*, 57:4, Summer, 1968, 601-603.

Johnson, Richard A., 'Summer Knowledge, Hard Hours' [joint review of *THH* and Delmore Schwartz, *Selected Poems: Summer Knowledge*], *The Sewanee Review*, 76:4, Autumn 1968, 682-685.

Sheehan, Donald, 'Varieties of Technique: Seven Recent Books of American Poetry, *Contemporary Literature* 10:2, Spring 1969, 298-301.

Perloff, Marjorie, 'Anthony Hecht, The Hard Hours', *The Far Point*, 2, 1969, 45-51.

SEVEN AGAINST THEBES (1973)

Dimmock, G.E., jr., *The Yale Review*, 63, Summer 1974, 573-590,

Lloyd-Jones, Hugh, 'Tragedy in Modern Verse', *The Times Literary Supplement*, November 1, 1974, 1221.

MILLIONS OF STRANGE SHADOWS (1977)

Rowe, Portis, *Library Journal*, 102, March 1, 1977, 611.

Donoghue, Denis, 'Millions of Strange Shadows', *New York Times Book Review*, March 27, 1977, 6-7.

Elliott, George P., 'The Freshness of the Text', *The Times Literary Supplement*, 3: 921, May 6, 1977, 548.

Madoff, Steven, 'The Poet at Cross Purposes', *The Nation*, 225, September 3, 1977, 188-190.

Porter, Peter, 'What's become of Browning?', *The Observer*, October 2, 1977.

Sealy, Douglas, 'Recent Poetry', *The Irish Times*, October 10, 1977.

Enright, D.J., 'Dirge of Birth', *The Listener*, November 17, 1977.

Howard, Richard, 'Shadows', *Poetry*, 131, November 1977, 103-6; reprinted in his *Alone With America: Essays on the Art of Poetry in the United States Since 1950*, Atheneum, New York, 1980, 164-73.

Bloom, Harold, 'Harold Bloom on Poetry', *New Republic*, November 26, 1977, 25.

Crossley-Holland, Kevin, *Ambit*, 74, 1977.

Murray, G.E., *The Georgia Review*, 31, Winter 1977, 962-971.

Renchler, R.S., *Prairie Schooner*, 51, Winter 1977-1978, 416-417.

Falck, Colin, *The New Review*, 4:45-46, December 1977 / January 1978, 70-72 .

London Magazine, May 1978.

Ehrenpreis, Irvin, 'At the Poles of Poetry', *The New York Review of Books*, 25, August 17, 1978, 48-50.

Crick, Philip, *Samphire*, 3:2, Summer 1978.

Unsigned, *English Studies*, 59:5, 1978, 465.

Graham, Desmond, 'The Lying Art?', *Stand*, 20:1, 1978-1979, 65-71.

THE VENETIAN VESPERS (1979)

Ricks, Christopher, 'Poets Who Have Learned Their Trade', *New York Times Book Review*, December 2, 1979, 1, 44-45
Pettingell, Phoebe, 'Anthony Hecht's Transmutations', *New Leader*, 62:24, December 17, 1979, 22-23.
Grosholz, Emily, *The Hudson Review*, 33:2, Spring 1980, 293-308.
Keates, Jonathan, 'Vault Echoes', *The Spectator*, 244:7922, May 10, 1980, 23-4.
Garfitt, Roger. 'Contrary Attractions', *The Times Literary Supplement*, 4027, May 30, 1980, 623.
Motion, Andrew, 'Veils and Veins', *New Statesman*, 99, May 1980, 717.
Bedient, Calvin, 'New Confessions', *The Sewanee Review*, 88:3, 1980, 474-488.
Brownjohn, Alan, *Encounter*, 55:5, 1980, 64-70.
Davie, Donald, 'The Twain Not Meeting', *Parnassus*, 8:1, 1980, 84-91.
Graham, D., *Stand*, 22:1, 1980, 73-79.
McClatchy, J.D., 'Summaries and Evidence', *Partisan Review*, 47:4, 1980, 639-44.
Malahat Review, 54, 1980, 153.
Shetley, Vernon, 'Take But Degree Away', *Poetry*, 137:5, February 1981, 297-302.
Gioia, Dana, 'Three Poets in Mid-Career', *The Southern Review*, 17:3, 1981, 667-674.
Tripp, Y, *Poetry Wales*, 16:3, 1981, 102-104.
Howard, B., *Prairie Schooner*, 55:4, Winter 1981-1982, 84-89.

OBBLIGATI (1986)

Publisher's Weekly, 229, June 13, 1986, 64.
Guillory, Daniel L., *Library Journal*, 3, August 1986.
Thwaite, Anthony, *Washington Post, Book World*, August 31, 1986.
Menand, Louis, 'A Metaphor Is a Terrible Thing to Waste', *New York Times Book Review*, 91, September 7, 1986, 19+.
Pritchard, William H., 'Formal Measures', *New Republic*, 195, December 15 1986, 37-39.
Dostert, Candyce, *Wilson Library Bulletin*, 61:4, December 1986, 71-72.
Hadas, Rachel, *Partisan Review*, 54:3, Summer 1987, 493-497.
Pratt, W., *World Literature Today*, 61:2, 1987, 289.
Beaver, H., *Parnassus*, 14:2, 1988, 189-195.
Dickinson Studies, 66, 1988, 27-28.

COLLECTED EARLIER POEMS (1990)

Logan, William, *New York Times Book Review*, July 1990, 26.
Forbes, Peter, 'Visions of a Junkyard', *The Independent*, July 6, 1991.
Mackinnon, Lachlan, 'A Wordsworthian Gift: Moral Pilgrimage in the Poetry of Anthony Hecht', *The Times Literary Supplement*, 4608, July 26, 1991, 4.
Whitworth, John, 'First Division Material', *The Spectator*, November 16, 1991.
Forbes, Peter, 'Books of the Year', *The Independent*, November 23, 1991.
Toibin, Colm, 'Books of the Year', *The Irish Times*, November 30, 1991.

V.F., *Ore*, 43, 1991, 41-42.
Virginia Quarterly Review, 67:2, 1991, 63-64.
Panabaker, J., *Queens Quarterly*, 98:1, 1991, 250-252.
Unsigned, *The New Welsh Review*, 17, August 1992.
Anselman, R.A., 'Poet's Choice', *Papers on Language and Literature*, 33, 1997, 13.
Taylor, J., *Poetry*, 170, 1997, 70.

THE TRANSPARENT MAN (1990)

Logan, William, *New York Times Book Review*, July 1990, 26.
Pettingell, Phoebe, 'Anthony Hecht's Designs', *The New Leader*, 73, October 1-15, 1990, 19-20.
The New York Times Book Review, 95, July 22, 1990, 26-27.
Nuttall, Jeff, 'Bookends', *Time Out*, June 19, 1991.
Forbes, Peter, 'Visions of a Junkyard', *The Independent*, July 6, 1991.
Mackinnon, Lachlan, 'A Wordsworthian Gift: Moral Pilgrimage in the Poetry of Anthony Hecht', *The Times Literary Supplement*, 4608, July 26, 1991, 4.
Jennings, Elizabeth, 'Elizabeth Jennings's Poetry Guide', *The Daily Telegraph*, August 17, 1991.
Whitworth, John, 'First Division Material', *The Spectator*, November 16, 1991.
Taylor, H., T*he Southern Review*, 27, Winter 1991, 435-442.
Stevenson, Anne, 'Passacaglias of Pain', *Poetry Review*, 81:1, 1991, 6-7.
V.F., *Ore*, 43, 1991, 41-42.
Unsigned, *The New Welsh Review*, 17, August 1992.
Panabaker, J., *Queens Quarterly*, 98:1, 1992, 250-252.

THE HIDDEN LAW (1993)

Porter, Peter, 'The Magician and the Censor', *Poetry Review*, 83:4, January 1993, 4-8.
Taylor, Robert, 'Master of Disguise', *The Boston Globe,* April 4, 1993.
Parady, Neil, 'Easily Missed', *The Guardian,* April 6, 1993.
Holm, D.K., 'Poets Cornered', *Williamette Week*, April 1-7, 1993.
Jenkins, Nicholas, 'The Making of Two Poets', *The Times Literary Supplement*, 4697, April 9, 1993, 10.
Marsack, Robyn, *Scotland on Sunday*, April 11, 1993.
Hamilton, Ian, 'God and the Poems of W.H. Auden', *The Sunday Telegraph*, April 18, 1993.
'New and Recommended', *The Boston Globe*, April 25 ,1993.
Howard, Richard, 'The Sage of Anxiety', *Washington Post, Book World*, April 25, 1993.
Davison, Peter, 'A Companionship of Poets', *The Atlantic*, 271, April 1993, 128-131.
Kessler, Edward, 'W.H. Auden's Transforming Experience', *The Washington Times*, May 2, 1993.
MacKendrick, L.K., *Choice*, July / August 1993.
Eakin, Emily, 'In Short', *New York Times Book Review*, August 15, 199, 18.
'Noted', *Bostonia*, Summer 1993.
Jensen, Kurt, 'Books', *Seattle Weekly*, November 10, 1993.
Donnelly, Daria, 'A Poet's Poet', *Commonweal*, 120, December 17, 1993, 18-19.
'University Press Paperbacks', *The Washington Times*, March 27, 1994.

'New in Paperback', *The Washington Post, Book World*, April 3, 1994.
Boly, John R., *Journal of English and Germanic Philology*, 93:2, April, 1994, 265-267.
Burris, Sidney, 'Reading Hecht Reading Auden', *The Southern Review*, 30:2, Spring 1994, 364-370.
Forum for Modern Language Studies, August 1994.
Bright, Michael, 'Auden's Poetry', *English Language in Transition*, 37:2, 1994, 231-234.
Spears, Monroe K., 'Auden Twenty Years After A Question Of Poetic Justice', *The Sewanee Review*, 102:3, Summer 1994, 476-482.
Speirs, L., 'New Writing Drama and Poetry', *English Studies*, 74:2, 1994, 74:2.
Guillory, Daniel, 'The Hidden Law', *Magill's Literary Annual*, 1994.
Unsigned, *The Virginia Quarterly Review*, 70:4, 1994, A122.
Tillinghast, Richard, 'W.H. Auden: 'Stop All the Clocks', *The Gettysburg Review*, 8:3, Summer 1995, 425-435.

ON THE LAWS OF THE POETIC ART (1995)

Lynch, Bryan, *The Irish Times*, July 15, 1995.
Davison, Peter, 'The Rules of the Game', *Boston Book Review*, September 1995.
Slavitt, D.R., *The New England Review*, 17:4, Fall 1995, 150-154.
Kirby, D., *Library Journal*, 120:10, 1995, 114.
Logan, William, 'On Poetry', *Washington Post, Book World*, February 25 ,1996.
Ford, Mark, untitled, *The Times Literary Supplement*, 4849, March 8, 1996, 28.
Vendler, Helen, 'Worth a Thousand Words?', *The New York Review of Books*, 43:8, May 9, 1996, 39-42.
Beum, Robert, 'Anthony Hecht on Poetic Art', *The Sewanee Review*, 104:1, 1996, 158-163.
Quinn, J., *Poetry Review*, 86:2, 1996, 73.
Virginia Quarterly Review, 72:1, 1996, 14.
Sell, Roger D., *Review of English Studies,* New Series, 48:190, May 1997, 287-288.
Clausen, Christopher, *Comparative Literature Studies,* 34:2, 1997, 191-193.
Antioch Review, 55, 1997, 134.

FLIGHT AMONG THE TOMBS (1996)

Christian, Graham, *Library Journal*, October 1, 1996.
Seaman, Donna, *Booklist*, November 11, 1996.
McClatchy, J.D., 'Poet Finds Words for the Unspeakable', *Washington Times Books*, December 22, 1996.
Logan, William, 'Old Guys', *The New Criterion*, 15:4, December 1996, 61-69.
Gioia, Dana, *Poetry, Washington Post, Book World*, January 26, 1997.
Bayley, John, 'Living Ghosts', *The New York Review of Books*, 44:5, March 27, 1997, 18-21.
Aaron, Jonathan, *Boston Sunday Globe*, March 30, 1997.
Yenser, Stephen, 'Poetry in Review', *The Yale Review*, 85, 161-176, April 1997.
Thwaite, Anthony 'Poets Behaving Playfully', *The Sunday Telegraph*, June 15, 1997.
Mackinnon, Lachlan, 'American Poetry', *The Independent*, August 9, 1997.
Montefiore, Janet, 'As Polished as Georgian Cutlery', *The Times Literary Supplement*, 4295, August 22, 1997, 24.

Haines, John, 'Poetry Chronicle', *The Hudson Review*, 50:2, Summer 1997, 317-324.
Hollander, John, 'On Anthony Hecht', *Raritan*, 17:1, 140-151, Summer 1997.
Kendall, Tim, 'Poetry in Brief', *The Guardian*, August 28, 1997, G2, 13.
Oser, Lee, *World Literature Today*, 71, 594, Summer 1997.
Sail, Lawrence, 'Death's Disguises', *Poetry Review* (London), 87:3, Autumn 1997, 73-74.
Byard, Olivia, 'Paradise Illustrated and Many Deaths Foretold', *Oxford Times*, October 10, 1997, 21.
Josipovici, Gabriel, 'Books of the Year', *The Independent*, November 29, 1997.
Taylor, J., *Poetry*, 170:3, 1997, 172-174.
Josipovici, Gabriel, 'International Books of the Year', *The Times Literary Supplement*, 4940, 1997, 13.
Foy, John, 'The Marriage of Logic and Desire: Some Reflections on Form', *Parnassus*, 23:1, 287-308, 1998.

ANTHONY HECHT IN CONVERSATION WITH PHILIP HOY (1999)

Pursglove, Glyn, 'Poetry Comment', *Acumen*, 35, September, 1999, p. 114.
Clark, Heather, 'Revising Intention', *Thumbscrew*, 15, Winter-Spring, 2000, 75-77.
Latané, David, 'Fresh Woods, Pastures New', *Stand*, New Series, 2:2, June, 2000, 69-71.
Crotty, Patrick, 'Poets on the Parrish', *The Times Literary Supplement*, October 27, 2000, p. 27.
Share, D., *Essays in Criticism*, 50:4, October, 2000, 378-383.

DISSERTATIONS

German, Norman H., '"What Do We Know Of Lasting?" Renewal of Perception and Reanimation of the World in the Works of Anthony Hecht', *Dissertation Abstracts International*, 44:2, August 1983, 489A, Ann Arbor, Michigan.
Lindsay, Geoffrey, 'Dramatic Strategies in the Poetry of Robert Lowell, Richard Howard and Anthony Hecht', University of Toronto, *Dissertation Abstracts International*, 53:12, June 1993, Ann Arbor, Michigan, 4322A.
Tung, Charles Man Fong, 'Poetic Witness', M.Phil Thesis, Faculty of English Language and Literature, University of Oxford, 1994, 86pp.

ARCHIVES
with holdings of A.H.'s correspondence

Bishop, Elizabeth, Papers 1925-1979, New York State Historical Documents, Vassar College Library, Special Collections, Poughkeepsie, New York.
Finkel, Donald, Papers 1947-1983, Washington University Libraries, St. Louis, Missouri.
Gass, William H., Papers 1948-1981, Washington University Libraries, St. Louis, Missouri.
Hardwick, Elizabeth, Papers 1934-1991, Harry Ransom Humanities Research Center, University of Texas, Austin, Texas.
Justice, Donald, Papers 1936-1998, Special Collections Department, University of Delaware Library, Newark, Delaware.

Mahon, Derek, Papers 1979-1994, Emory University, Special Collections Department, Robert W. Woodruff Library, Atlanta, Georgia.

Moss, Howard, Papers 1935-1987, New York Public Library, Rare Books and Manuscripts, Berg Collection, New York.

Nemerov, Howard, Papers 1939-1985, Washington University Libraries, St Louis, Missouri.

Palaemon Press, Winston-Salem, North Carolina, Editorial Archive 1974-1984, Brown University, John Hay Library.

Sexton, Anne, Papers 1912-1996, Harry Ransom Research Center, University of Texas, Austin, Texas.

Simic, Charles, Papers, Milne Special Collections and Archives, University of New Hampshire Library, Durham, New Hampshire.

Sissman, L.E., Papers 1944-1981, Houghton Library, Harvard University, Cambridge, Massachusetts.

Tate, Allen, Tate Collection, Princeton University Library, Princeton, New Jersey.

Van Duyn, Mona, Papers 1942-1985, Washington University Libraries, St Louis, Missouri.

Wright, James, Papers, Kenyon College Library, Gambier, Ohio.

THE HECHT ARCHIVES

Hecht's papers were recently purchased by Emory University in Georgia, and are expected to be available to researchers by early 2005. The holding, whose reference code is MSS926, measures approximately 50 linear feet, and contains writings by Hecht, writings by others, correspondence, personal files, academic material, subject files, and audio-visual material. Inquiries should be sent to:

The Coordinator, Arrangement and Description Unit,
Special Collections & Archives Division,
Robert W. Woodruff Library,
Emory University
540 Asbury Circle,
Atlanta,
Georgia 30322-2870,
U.S.A.

T: + (404) 727-6887
F: + (404) 727-0360

The Critics

'A baroque exuberance in the medium characterizes Hecht's poetry; the words whirl and perform their curves ...'

Joseph Bennet, review of *A Summoning of Stones*, 1954

'If Hecht, often disturbed by disorder and death, is drawn by ideal proportion, elegance and colour ... he is yielding to promptings that at his age only a fanatically serious spectator would deny him.'

Louise Bogan, review of *A Summoning of Stones*, 1954

'Whatever the tactic – and his approaches are many – the strategy is basically the same: Hecht works against the grain, but so smoothly that we almost fail to notice. He gives us valved emotion; rather than direct expression of feeling, he presents, in a magnificent variety of forms, the artifices we construct in the face of our historical and biological condition. Thus we get both formal brilliance and intense, often bitter, irony – and, more difficult to trace, a humane and kindly sympathy for man, inadequate as he struggles against destruction.'

Richard A. Johnson, comment on *The Hard Hours*, 1968

'We have gotten into the bad habit of ranking our poets. I refuse to do this. I can only say that whoever else may be at the top, Hecht is there too; for there is nobody better.'

Allen Tate, comment on *The Hard Hours*, 1968

'... Hecht's voice is his own, but his language, more amply than that of any other living poet writing in English, derives from, adds to, is part of the great tradition. Formerly, this would scarcely have been worth remarking on at any length. But in this age many poets, including some important ones, turn their backs on high culture, vandalize the past, see in history "me" and "now", fracture or flatten language, find sublimity, if anywhere, only in the darkest depths.'

George P. Elliott, review of *Millions of Strange Shadows*, 1977

'[Hecht] has in many ways carried forward and modified a kind of tradition that I associate mainly with Tate and Auden, the leading members of the second generation of modernists (if we have Stevens, Pound, and Eliot in the first generation). He has dealt with the terrible divisiveness of the age with an extraordinary honesty and grace – what Auden called for in 'The Shield of Achilles'. My sense of the current scene is that his kind of poetry will matter a great deal more from now on, after a period of rather shameless opportunism, and what is so reassuring is that he is writing better than ever.'

Ashley Brown, 'The Poetry of Anthony Hecht', 1978

'A beautifully wrought book, without a false note. Hecht's poems should be treated as sacred objects. Reading them tends to make other poets feel clumsy; they should be hung on walls for the wit is immaculate, the accomplishment thrilling, the choice of word piercing.'

Alastair Reid, review of *Millions of Strange Shadows*, 1979

'Lexiconish, detached, deliberate, Hecht can leave a short poem still cold or spinning with pedantic fanciness, but in his longer poems – a great new direction for him – a ground bass of sober feeling begins to hum and grow ever more insistent until it is frightening.

Calvin Bedient, review of *The Venetian Vespers*, 1980

'Alastair Reid has said: "Hecht's poems should be treated as sacred objects." This is fulsome; but Hecht has let it be quoted on his dust jacket, and it's soon apparent that in this as in previous collections Hecht does indeed write poems in the hope that, as Reid goes on to say, "they should be hung on walls." They are all, in one way or another, *framed*, held off at a distance from the life that they feed on and undoubtedly in some sense mirror.'

Donald Davie, review of *The Venetian Vespers*, 1980

'Hecht's deployment of the English language can only be described as gorgeous.'

Emily Grosholz, review of *The Venetian Vespers*, 1980

'Through the four decades of his literary career, Anthony Hecht has shown himself to belong not only to that small group of contemporary American poets whose work is truly accomplished but also to that still smaller group whose members have discovered some individual, rewarding way to dwell upon the special horrors of the age. Hecht's approach in poem after poem has been measured and thoughtful, avoiding the reciprocal temptations of self-pity and (the more dangerous because the less frequently condemned) of self-congratulation at his own toughness. But if he comes at his subject directly, he does not do so lightly armed. Most of his work is "formal" in both senses – elevated and patterned. He is probably the grandest of our contemporary poets in tone and dignity. With his ramified syntax, his amplitudinous, Latinate vocabulary, and his readiness to retrieve words and constructions that verge on archaism, he presents a voice of unexampled refinement.'

Brad Leithauser, 'Poet for a Dark Age', 1986

'Anthony Hecht is, without question, the best poet writing in English today. If I am not willing to lavish superlatives on him, it is neither because of the considerations of good

taste, nor because of a foreigner's natural prudence with epithets; it's simply because on the heights this poet inhabits there is no hierarchy.'

Joseph Brodsky, 'Anthony Hecht and the Art of Poetry', 1989

'"Who indeed knows how best to think about victims?" asks the political philosopher Judith Shklar, since they are so very likely to be regarded untruthfully, to be made to serve the onlooker's pleasure and anxiety. It is a question crucial to a poetry so haunted by the fact, the memory and spectacle of the Holocaust. So one might observe that even in a poem like "Rites and Ceremonies", Hecht's one extended work on the subject ... there is a deep resistance to moralization or melodrama, even to gestures of mourning. To witness, even to relive, are acts that require of the writer a discipline of both plainness and surprise ...'

Kenneth Gross, 'Hecht and the Imagination of Rage', 1989

'I first discovered *The Hard Hours* as a freshman in college when I wandered into the poetry section of the campus bookstore and somewhat haphazardly picked it off the shelf along with a few other books whose titles attracted me. I have forgotten the other books, but I was immediately arrested by the voice in *The Hard Hours* – its low, plaintive, apocalyptic urgency, its wry irony and unmistakable anguish. I took the book home and didn't so much read as devour it. The poems seemed haunted, puzzling, necessary. They fused the personal and the political in radical ways; they cried out in the wilderness to be heard. Sometimes they were playful, knowing, cynical; other times they summoned up the most horrific human experiences with a cool, dispassionate fury. Informed by what one of the poems defined as a necessary "Comic sense", they also testified to the darkest aspect of our natures. One listened to the naked suffering in such poems as "More Light! More Light!", "Rites and Ceremonies", and "Behold the Lilies of the Field", and was never quite the same afterward.'

Edward Hirsch, 'Comedy and Hardship', 1989

'The strictest metrist of them all, Hecht would seem superficially to have continued unchanged the Eliot-Ransom line in which he began, for even in his most recent work he continues his characteristic use of intricate metrical organization and crossed rhymes that make his stanzas look like seventeenth-century poems. Yet Anthony Hecht is not, and never was, merely a conventional versifier. He combines a metaphysical style with a keen play of language and an attitude to experience that makes his work unmistakably his own. The ironies in his superbly crafted poems are not merely verbal, for Hecht is a modern man who believes in God and whose view of American life is not, like those of the Whitman-inspired, optimistic. In the midst of inescapable discrepancies between what we expect of life and what experience gives us, Hecht is open to sensuous pleasures; the very texture of his versing is a play of sound, a search for aural consonances that doubly delight the mind and the ear. But at the core of his poetry there is a Hebraic stoicism in the presence of immitigable fate.'

Daniel Hoffman, 'Our Common Lot', 1989

'[Hecht] is a contemplative rather than a lyrical poet. A steady contemplation of things in their order and worth — the facts of his own life, the course of history, the archive of myth and belief — is his goal. And it is, in Santayana's phrase, the truth that absorbs him and carries him along: a wary, circumscribed, but certain knowledge on which are erected love's monuments, and hope's ideal cities, and all the bright, revolving orders of the imagination. But he indulges their excesses precisely in order to test and often to undermine them. They are his rough magic, and he will abjure them.'

J.D. McClatchy, *Anatomies of Melancholy*, 1989

'But although X [the speaker in "The Venetian Vespers"] is saying, in his way, that he is one of the hollow men of our time, the poem he figures in is anything but empty. He may be a fiasco, but the poem about him is a triumph. What he says may be dispiriting, but the way he says it is rich in splendours we can treasure. In the words of Hippolyta, after Theseus has given his little talk on poetry (and in a time when "admirable" meant "to be marvelled at"), it is a work which "grows to something of great constancy, / But – howsoever – strange and admirable."'

John Frederick Nims, 'Drenched in Fine Particulars', 1989

'Hecht belongs only in part to that civilized tradition represented in our century chiefly by T.S. Eliot and thereafter by John Crowe Ransom, Allen Tate, and Robert Lowell. He is only half assimilated to what Matthew Arnold called Hellenism. His other half is emphatically a Jew. His is the high culture of those post-enlightenment German Jews whose glorious error was to believe in the ideals of German/European culture more than their hosts did. Among his relatively recent poetic ancestors we may think of that classic Jew, that tormented wit, that romantic sceptic, that exalted and profane lyricist Heinrich Heine. Among his ancient fathers is the author of Lamentations; as Babylon to Jeremiah, so Buchenwald to Hecht. At its most energetic and disturbing, then, Hecht's art registers a Hellenic delight in beauty and order undermined by the Hebraic conviction that the beauty and order of high culture have been founded on suffering and cruelty.'

Alicia Ostriker, 'Hecht as Gentile and Jew', 1989

'Anthony Hecht's poetry has deservedly been admired for its mastery of form, a mastery rarely found in American poetry of the last three decades. Yet even among those who do not write formal poetry Hecht stands with the yet more distinguished few whose work goes beyond virtuosity or formal elegance to meditate upon the very conditions that give rise to its formality – conditions or rather *imperatives* that may challenge and perhaps in extreme cases almost subvert the poet's finest accomplishments.'

Peter Sacks, 'Anthony Hecht's "Rites and Ceremonies":
Reading *The Hard Hours*', 1989

'From virtually the first page of *A Summoning of Stones* ... to the last of *The Venetian Vespers* ... Hecht asks one continual question: "What's become of Paradise?" ... The question reflects neither Yeatsian nostalgia for vanished orders nor regret for the loss of pastoral realms and innocent, childlike pleasures; rather, it contains a deeper moral dimension, often dismissed or ignored by pastoralists who also look back regretfully but only sensuously. Hecht's province is the loss of ethical innocence and the ontogeny of evil. For paradises are lost, in his world, as a result of human sin, not error. The perennial religious question, *unde malum*, has yielded to him, in thirty years of poetry, no easy answers.'

Willard Spiegelman, *The Didactic Muse*, 1989

'For an author known for his erudition and technique, Hecht's final lesson may seem surprising. I think it's something like this: that the quality of one's writing, like the quality of one's life, depends directly on the depth of one's human concern.'

Norman Williams, 'Poetic Devises', 1989

'Some poets are saved by grace, others by will. Mr Hecht began as a poet of convenience and charm, of difficult form and baroque extravagance ... Scarred by a history whose lessons will be ignored, and whose lessons will murder us, he has become our only poet who is able to horrify ... The beauty of his language is stilled by the horror of knowledge.'

William Logan, review of *Collected Earlier Poems* and *The Transparent Man*, 1990

'Anthony Hecht is one of the best poets now writing ... It is time for the startling, unostentatious originality of his work to be celebrated beyond a small world of isolated ardent connoisseurs.'

Lachlan Mackinnon, review of *Collected Earlier Poems* and *The Transparent Man*, 1991

'*The Transparent Man* is a brilliant and moving collection of poems by a master of what, these days, one might call the Old School of American verse. The fancy-work will not be to everyone's taste. Nor, I suspect, will Hecht escape sneers from poets who dislike philosophical moralizing. For this reviewer, however, Hecht is still a model poet, an artist of integrity and insight whose gift of grace is strengthened by a fearless, utterly unhysterical recognition of horror.'

Anne Stevenson, review of *The Transparent Man*, 1991

'This is a book about poetry, about a poet who was dedicated to the art like few others of our time, whose poetic technique only another poet as gifted as Hecht could gloss ... The richness of reference in this book to history, prosody, theology, poetry, punctuation, makes for a long swim in the heady liquor of poetry – not only Auden's poetry but that of the hundreds of authors whom Auden read ... It is a pleasure to read.'

Peter Davison, review of *The Hidden Law*, 1993

'I know of no other instance of a poet of comparable mastery of his art and his experience taking up in such loving detail the work of a predecessor (and near contemporary).'

Richard Howard, review of *The Hidden Law*, 1993

'The Hidden Law ... is not just a meditation on Auden, but on Fate as well. Hecht has made brilliant use of mask and fantasy to broach painful questions in his poems, and The Hidden Law's dispassionate critical voice unfolds a powerful meditation on the vicissitudes of the poetic life. An expert in what he once called the "saline latitudes of incontinent grief", Hecht returns repeatedly to the disappointment he detects in Auden's later years ...Wilde described criticism as "the record of one's own soul", and this is the underlying pressure at work in The Hidden Law, much as it was in Auden's own huge A Certain World ... As the terminal point 1955 suggests, The Hidden Law is at its most significant level a narrative of Anthony Hecht's emergence as a poet, and for all that the book tells us by implication, it takes its place alongside MacNeice's Yeats and Berryman's Crane.'

Nicholas Jenkins, review of The Hidden Law, 1993

'Anthony Hecht is one of America's most rigorously formal poets, but his criticism is oddly ill disciplined and shapeless. His study of W.H. Auden, The Hidden Law ... contained all sorts of excellent perceptions, yet few workable, clear-cut categories, and certainly no hidden laws. The title of Hecht's A.W. Mellon lectures again seems to promise some firm universal precepts: the six talks turn out, however, to be a boggy morass of aesthetic enthusiasms and tentative speculations loosely gathered under a series of catch-all headings ...'

Mark Ford, review of On The Laws of the Poetic Art, 1996

'Anthony Hecht's majestic development into a great poet has progressed across half a century. Flight Among the Tombs is his poignant and ironic masterpiece ... Few poets stand with Henry James and Marcel Proust: John Crowe Ransom, W.H. Auden, James Merrill, and Anthony Hecht are in that company.'

Harold Bloom, comment on Flight Among the Tombs, 1997

'On the whole, however, these deadly monologues do not, despite their variety, energy and assurance, show the poet at his best. Anthony Hecht has always been much possessed by death, but whereas his deservedly famous "Consider the lilies" or "More light! More light!" took real horrors, unsparingly and compassionately, in order to examine them, here the cruelty lies less in the poems' matter than in their manner.'

Janet Montefiore, review of Flight Among the Tombs, 1997

'There are times when the sheer gorgeousness of his descriptions can verge on the hypnotic, as in the appropriately titled "Là-bas: A Trance", or weave a spell of "damasked language" (a phrase from "Death the Poet") that might seem to be its own justification. All the more interesting, then, that in fine poems in memory of James Merrill and Joseph Brodsky, Hecht weighs affectionate homage and the power of art against the helplessness induced by real loss.'

Lawrence Sail, review of Flight Amongst the Tombs, 1997